Hidden Survivors: Portraits of Poor Jews in America

BOOKS BY THOMAS J. COTTLE

Time's Children
The Abandoners
The Present of Things Future (with Stephen L. Klineberg)
The Prospect of Youth
Perceiving Time
Out of Discontent (with Craig R. Eisendrath and
        Laurence Fink)
The Voices of School
College: Reward and Betrayal
A Family Album
Black Children, White Dreams
Private Lives and Public Accounts
Busing
Children in Jail
Adolescent Psychology: Contemporary Perspectives
Barred From School
Human Adjustment (with Phillip Whitten)
Black Testimony
Children's Secrets
Psychotherapy: Current Perspectives
        (with Phillip Whitten)
Hidden Survivors: Portraits of Poor Jews in America

HIDDEN SURVIVORS

Portraits of Poor Jews in America

Thomas J. Cottle

Prentice-Hall, Inc., Englewood Cliffs, New Jersey

The author is grateful to the following publications:

Portions of Chapter 1 first appeared as "Cranepool the Janitor" in *New Society*, London, the weekly review of the social sciences, © copyright *New Society* 1978.

Portions of Chapters 1, 2, 4, and 5 originally appeared in *MOMENT* Magazine.

Book design by Joan Ann Jacobus
Art Director: Hal Siegel

Hidden Survivors: Portraits of Poor Jews in America
Copyright © 1980 by Thomas J. Cottle

Printed in the United States of America
Prentice-Hall International, Inc., London/Prentice-Hall of Australia, Pty. Ltd., Sydney/Prentice-Hall of Canada, Ltd., Toronto/Prentice-Hall of India Private Ltd., New Delhi/Prentice-Hall of Japan, Inc., Tokyo/Prentice-Hall of Southeast Asia Pte. Ltd., Singapore/Whitehall Books Limited, Wellington, New Zealand
10 9 8 7 6 5 4 3 2 1

Library of Congress Cataloging in Publication Data
Cottle, Thomas J
    Hidden survivors.
    Includes bibliographical references.
    1. Jews in the United States—Social conditions—Case studies.
2. Poor—United States—Case studies. 3. Aged—United States—Case studies. 4. United States—Social conditions—1960-   —Case studies.
I. Title.
E184.J5C67   305.2'6   79-26718
ISBN 0-13-387357-9

To the memory of Joseph and Sonya Weinstock
and Louis and Rachel Cottle

Acknowledgments

Let me thank first the American Jewish Congress, and especially Arthur Hertzberg and Martin and Anne Peretz, whose generosity and encouragement helped to launch this work.

In addition, special thanks must go to Leonard Fein, Carol Kur, William Novack, Gerald M. Platt, Paul Barker, Michael I. Kessler, Paul Strudler, James Finn, Richard and Ruth Rogers, Eliot Liebow, Phillip Drysdale, Timothy Rutten, Sally Makacynas, Rosemary Daniels, Viviette Reynell, Jan Wallace, Ellen Levine, and to my editor, Mariana Fitzpatrick, for her encouragement and assistance in bringing this work to fruition.

My wife, Kay Cottle, our children, Claudia, Jason, and Sonya, and my parents, Gitta Gradova Cottle and Maurice H. Cottle, remain a constant source of love and support and a great deal more. So, too, do my grandparents, two of whom I barely remember, two of whom I never knew.

A last and heartfelt thank-you goes to the men and women who have participated in the research and who, by giving me permission to write about them, allowed me to share with them fragments of their lives.

Contents

Hidden Survivors: Portraits of Poor Jews in America

Introduction

In 1971, when researcher Ann G. Wolfe presented her paper "The Invisible Jewish Poor" to the annual meeting of the American Jewish Committee, many in the audience were shocked, others openly outraged. Poor Jews? In America? Were they hiding? And why hadn't someone been reporting their condition before? "We have blind spots in our vision of ourselves," Wolfe told her audience. "It is time to look at the facts."

My own exposure to the realities of America's elderly, impoverished Jews grew out of my long-standing work in America's poor communities. For seven years I worked closely with Jewish families in major metropolitan areas, existing in circumstances that can only be classified as poverty. Women and men mainly in their sixties and seventies, they live typically in old apartment houses or in some cases new housing projects built especially for the elderly by city or state governments. Some live on welfare, some live on meager Social Security benefits, some hold part-time jobs. All of those quoted here have granted permission for their words to appear in print. All names are fictitious.

In gathering my research I was to find that the facts of Jewish poverty are hard to come by. Philanthropic and social agencies are often the best source of such information, but as well meaning and capable as these agency workers may be, there simply is no way in which wholly accurate statistics on the subject of the Jewish poor can be ascertained. One fact that is known, however, is that Jewish poverty is not limited to the

Introduction

elderly, who are the subject of this book. It is estimated that men and women over sixty-five represent about 65 percent of the Jewish poor. But as we must constantly remind ourselves, these figures are at best calculated estimates. Further estimates on the subject suggest that the percent of American Jews living at or below the poverty level ranges from 12 to 19. As is true in all census information, the figures are at best an approximation, since the collection of census data is always difficult in the poorest communities. Still, even the lower range of the estimate may surprise those people who maintain the belief that Jews invariably reveal financial solvency if not outright affluence. This preconception is documented by the reaction of an ac- quaintance of mine, who should have known better, upon hearing of my work: "A book of poor Jews in the *United States*?" he remarked. "Where are you going to find them?"

Expressions having to do with Jews and money have been widespread in Western culture, owing in part to the notion that a portion of Jewish people have made financial successes of themselves and that Jews traditionally are associated with bank- ing and financial operations. The linking of Jews and wealth is an area in which prejudgments and stereotypes too often substi- tute for facts.

To those who would scoff at or overlook the reality of American Jews living in poverty, a few further statistics may prove enlightening:

To begin, a study conducted by the National Opinion Research Center of Chicago in 1962 reported that *15.3* percent of Jewish households revealed incomes of less than $3,000 a year. The figure is almost identical for Catholic families; Pro- testants show 22.7 percent living at this income level. As we have noted, approximately 65 percent of poor Jews were be- tween the ages of sixty and sixty-five. (About 18 percent of America's Jews are sixty-five and over.) Furthermore, while the figures are imprecise, it was estimated that over 60 percent of the elderly live alone.

2

If some of us remain blind to the existence of the Jewish poor, so do we fail to observe those areas of cities where a high proportion of the Jewish poor reside. Perhaps our blind spot is caused by the familiar statistic indicating that the median income for heads of Jewish families a decade ago was $6,000, or some $2,000 more than the figure for the general public. Nonetheless, cities like New York, Miami, and Los Angeles, where the common stereotype holds that most Jews live in affluence, reveal serious pockets of Jewish poverty. Ten years ago, the South Beach area of Miami, for example, listed a population of more than 40,000 people, 80 percent of whom were over sixty-five. Eighty-five percent of those people were Jews showing an average annual income of less than $2,500. Similarly, Los Angeles reported almost 9,000 Jews receiving some form of public assistance. In New York it has been estimated—for few valid statistics on the subject are available—that 350,000 Jews live at or below the poverty level.

According to Bernard Warach of the New York Association for Services for the Aged,* 13 percent, or 780,000, of America's 6 million Jews are older people. Approximately one half of these elderly people live at or below the so-called official government-determined poverty line ($3,100 for one person living in an urban center). Another one quarter of that group of elderly people live in families earning $4,000 a year or less. In addition, Warach notes, some 100,000 to 200,000 Hasidic Jewish families reveal incomes of between $8,000 and $9,000. Finally, one finds approximately 100,000 divorced people, mainly women, and mentally impaired people with incomes of between $8,000 and $11,000. So in sum, data compiled as recently as 1978 confirm the study conducted by the National Opinion Research Center in 1962.†

*The association was founded in 1968 by the Federation of Jewish Philanthropies. The data cited here refer to 1978–1979.

†As national income statistics no longer are broken down by religion, data of this sort become increasingly difficult to collect.

Introduction

To be sure, characteristics of the elderly population are changing. Specifically, this group is becoming better educated and the recipient of increased pensions. Still, Jews tend to be averse to accepting public welfare grants, though not, obviously, straightforward entitlements. Elderly people, not so incidentally, may retain a savings of $1,500 per individual or $2,250 per couple and still be entitled to supplementary security benefits. This savings is usually set aside as a burial allowance.

In many respects, the Jewish poor experience the same problems encountered by those living in all poor communities. Unemployment is high, the housing is inadequate, health care often operates at the most minimal level, although there are exceptions, notably when a large hospital exists in a poor neighborhood. Moreover, there are shortages of food and relatively higher prices for it in the poorer community. There are also the intangibles: the discouragement, the loss of hope and faith, the feeling that one has been betrayed by the society, the government, by certain social service agencies, perhaps by one's own kind as well. And it is important to note that the particular problems facing the Jewish poor are compounded by the stereotypic notion that their presence, their very existence, is an anomaly. How can they be poor? they are asked. Surely something bizarre, unpredictable, caused them to be living among the poor. Surely they must have relatives, rich associates somewhere, who could bail them out of their circumstances. Even thoughtful, intelligent, and perceptive observers of American society, for example, remained unaware in the 1960s and 1970s of the poverty experienced by Hasidic Jews living in the well-known Williamsburg district of Brooklyn, New York. The "unusual" habits and traditions of the Hasidim were familiar, but the economic, social, political, and deeply personal transformations of this complex community were less well noted, even by some Jews.

The very same stereotype affects many Jews as well. How is it, they wonder, that they are obliged to go without and to feel, partly because of the common image of being a Jew, a special shame associated with poverty?

In spite of the lack of general awareness in this area, observations of the Jewish poor, and in particular the elderly Jewish poor, are hardly new endeavors. In fact, they constitute a relatively small body of the larger literature devoted to America's poverty, of which Michael Harrington's *The Other America* represents the best. *Home Life*, by Dorothy Rabinowitz and Yedida Nielsen, was a remarkable volume devoted to the lives of the elderly living in the proverbial old people's home. Irving Howe's colossal work *The World of Our Fathers* not only is required reading for those whose intellectual and personal concerns touch on the lives of America's Jews but must be singled out as a work that drew applause and warmth from a surprisingly huge worldwide audience. Not so incidentally, Barbara Myerhoff's recently published work *Number Our Days* follows in the well-grounded tradition of oral history and makes remarkable reading. Like Howe's book, the people are alive, history is alive; people's words and stories sanctify this fact.

A less well known piece about America's poor Jews was written in 1973 by Mark Effron, then a graduate student in Columbia University's School of Journalism. Treating the matter of Jewish poverty in New York's Lower East Side skillfully and in utterly human terms, Effron significantly titled his piece, "It Wasn't Supposed to Happen This Way." In its penultimate chapter, the author writes: "There is this city— this huge concrete and steel and garbage city which consumes lives. New York is an ambiguous lover. It promises riches. It steals them away. If this city is a dying proposition, the Lower East Side residents will die with it. It was this city which symbolized 'the American dream.' Now it is this city which typifies the American nightmare."*

---

*Mark Effron, "It Wasn't Supposed to Happen This Way." Unpublished manuscript, Columbia University, Graduate School of Journalism, 1973, page 54.

Not too many years after Effron wrote his piece, another New York writer, the very gifted seer and artist Paul Cowan, began publishing his pieces on New York's poor Jews in *The Village Voice*. Cowan's impressive capacity to capture the way life was led by those he chose as subjects for his portraits had a great effect on America's reading public. His powerful documentation of a serious social problem was greeted with the same surprise and sense of shock that Wolfe evoked several years earlier with her now-famous paper in Chicago.

It is important to note that the matter of America's poor Jews, and especially its elderly ones, is hardly an isolated, rarified piece of social history. It is part of a deeply complex history and evolution of social events. As we will note in greater detail in Chapter 9, Jewish poverty is intimately related to, if not a product of, years of immigration of Jews from numerous countries, as well as the social and political tensions that arose in the United States not only between Jews and Gentiles but between various ethnic and social class groupings of Jews themselves. One must recall, for example, that Eastern European and Western European Jews may have shared certain spiritual and historical elements, but in political and economic terms, they brought quite different attitudes, perceptions, and orientations to America. As Eliot Waldman reminds us: "Many of the Eastern European Jews who migrated to the United States had socialist leanings. This went against the vested interests of the capitalistic Jews who governed the Jewish charity boards. What actually developed was a division in Jewish culture. . . . In response to the attempt by the German Jews to acculturate their East European brethren, the new immigrants formed their own socialist trade unions, religious schools, Yiddish theater, congregations and charities."* Waldman goes on to cite a statement from the History of the United Hebrew Charities

*Eliot Waldman, "The Neighborhood Service Center: A Relook at Jewish Poverty." Unpublished manuscript, 1975, pages 3 and 4.

of the City of New York which bears repeating here if only to remind us of the variegated social and political histories of those people who may too quickly be clumped together as the elderly poor American Jew: "They [the Eastern European immigrants] were in general the more poorly equipped for a competitive struggle in industrial America, of all Jews who have arrived here. Their coming caused concern to the Jews already in this country, not only because of their prodigious numbers, but also because of the poverty of their background." In many respects, some of the same issues that dominated Jewish life at the turn of this century continue to haunt the descendants of those very people, the then new immigrants, and their brothers and sisters who were here to receive them. And it is in this historical spirit that the present book is conceived.

My own study of America's poor Jews is essentially based on conversations with a few people over a long period of time. Quantity of respondents is sacrificed, and with it, presumably, greater representation of the population in order to examine more closely the way life is led by a few people whose words constitute our living data and whose voices dramatize the struggle of a group to make itself felt in terms of its social problems. This struggle, common to many, has been enunciated by Herbert Blumer as follows: "The most casual observation and reflection shows clearly that the recognition by a society of its social problems is a highly selective process, with many harmful social conditions and arrangements not even making a bid for attention and with others falling by the wayside in what is frequently a fierce competitive struggle. Many push for societal recognition but only a few come out of the end of the funnel."*

Clearly this book is intended to enhance the process by which more and more people will emerge into the light.

*Herbert Blumer, "Social Problems As Collective Behavior." *Social Problems*, Winter 1971, Vol. 18, No. 3, page 302.

In this one instance, the relatively small sample of people presented in this book recalls a simple historical fact about the Jews where once again the number of people involved was surprisingly small. The first Jews to settle in America arrived here in 1654, not from Eastern or Western Europe, as is commonly believed, but from Brazil. The entire group of these refugees numbered twenty-three.

There is another small number about America's Jewry that also deserves comment, if only because it may justify a study wherein a tiny sample of people is being considered. As America enters the 1980s, there are still fewer than 10 million Jews in this land. Jews, in other words, continue to represent one of the smallest minorities. In some people's eyes, the number in fact is so small, not unlike the number of poor Jews, that it hardly seems worth writing about such a poorly represented minority. Surely such a small number would hardly claim the attention required to qualify their daily struggle, as Herbert Blumer said, as a genuinely meaningful social problem. More generally, however, the argument for taking seriously the history and destiny of so few people has sociological as well as personal roots.

In sociological terms, Jewish issues have inevitably elucidated conditions and problems within the greater society. "In studying America's Jews," Marshall Sklare wrote, "we are able to clarify the problem of the ethnic minority in modern society. While ethnic conflict in the United States centers on black-white confrontation rather than on Christian-Jewish tensions, the Jews still best exemplify the condition of being a minority group. . . . No matter how harmonious the relationship between Judaism and Christianity may appear, it is inherently a stressful relationship—the religions are closely related and historic rivals."*

Despite their minority status, the conditions of America's

*Marshall Sklare, *America's Jews*. New York: Random House, 1971, page 4.

poor Jews are not ineluctably depressing or hopeless. As the following pages attest, people do survive; their very words give us hope. Merely to listen to people who have survived an adverse history enhances our faith in life itself and our own ability to endure. The personal idiosyncratic life inevitably evolves amid the power of history and social order. Individual life stories and accounts testify to this fact. No individual, and importantly, no human group, is free of stresses caused in part by historical and social changes. "Life in an environment that permits cultural give and take," Solomon Grayzel wrote, "is bound to be hazardous for a minority. But the past two generations, like other periods in Jewish history, have demonstrated the possibility of attaining an integrated personality in which Judaism and western culture fuse harmoniously and creatively. There must be faith that the process will continue in the generations to come."*

A similar statement came from one of the people heard in this book. Yankel Kanter, a gentleman in his seventies, held my hand when he spoke the following words. It was late afternoon, I remember, of a day when, for various reasons, my own spirits were very low: "Go home, write your book about me, us, anybody you like. Don't look back and ask yourself does it make a difference to anyone; it's what you want to do. How do you know who'll read it, who'll think what about it? You got a job: Your job's to write. I got a job too. My job's to stay alive, for my sake, and your sake, too. If I die, look what I lose, and look what you lose, too. So we've both got a little interest in this book of yours. Now, the question is, will anybody else have an interest in what you and me have an interest in? Who knows? Who knows who'll read what? Who knows when you call out in pain if anybody will come and help you. Who knows if anybody ever hears you calling. You *don't* know. So you keep on

*Solomon Grayzel, *A History of the Contemporary Jews.* New York: Atheneum, 1977, pages 178–79.

living, and you keep on calling, and you keep on writing, and you wait, and you see what happens. Life gives no guarantees, you know. So you keep on going and you have faith. That's all, just faith. A lot of it if you're lucky, a little bit if you're not so lucky. But without it, *oi*, I don't even want to think about it. So have a little faith; we made it this far, who knows, tomorrow, God should only hear me, could be a little bit better."

One:

Housing:
Jacob and Millie Portman

The conception of a ghetto community in the United States has become such a popular and commonly used one, its meaning and validity are rarely questioned. In truth, it is very difficult, in many cases, to know what precisely a community is. What defines it? Are there clear-cut borders? Is it an anthropological, geographical, social, political term? Is there such a thing as a "pure" community, something that the residents of it could define and hold in their minds as a real entity? Furthermore, what is it that we mean by "ghetto"? Does the term imply that certain groups of people are obliged or choose to live close to each other, almost to the extent that people not within their designated social boundaries are excluded? And is it the case that those people living in what we call a ghetto are more in touch with one another, more intimate even in their daily encounters, than those of us who are said not to reside in ghettos?

Within most cities, poor Jews tend to cluster together. While the boundaries of their neighborhoods are not always clearly defined, there are instances when in fact a particular place marks the precise division between the Jews and, say, the Italians or Poles or Lithuanians. Needless to say, most neighborhoods are mixed ethnically to a far greater extent than our conceptions of these neighborhoods would indicate. Similarly, while the poor Jews may be said to live essentially in one or two or three major districts, it is also true that they are scattered throughout many poorer districts of cities like Philadelphia, New York, and Boston. In these districts, and one is loath to call them neighborhoods when the residents themselves may not use this word (the term "community" as it applies to a specific geographical region is rarely used), people reside in the all-too-familiar monuments of poverty.

The word "run-down" is used again and again to describe the older buildings where the Jews live, or once lived. In the past, the buildings, like the neighborhoods themselves, were pleasant enough, even handsome, and in some cases quite elegant. The buildings of anywhere from three to six or eight stories were strong, made of substantial materials, with complicated roof structures and large windows. The apartments in the front looked out over trees, or perhaps a small corner park, and while the buildings were constructed side by side so that each shared a common wall with its neighbor, they nonetheless provided some privacy and a sense that one's home was protected, secure.

Inside the apartments the facilities and fixtures, the doors and windows, floors and ceilings were often handsomely designed and executed with care and taste. Wood was used in abundance and walls were frequently covered with striking papers. Elaborate wall lights and chandeliers were in every room; even the enormous entrances and stairwells were beautifully lit, providing an inviting spatial overture to the rooms that lay beyond and above.

Today these same buildings are drab and shabby. The fixtures are gone, the wallpaper is peeling, if not pulled away, wood has been painted over, mostly a dirty white. Large spaces have been converted to small ones, spacious living rooms have been partitioned off into three and four bedrooms. Kitchen and pantry areas have become bedrooms and sitting rooms, closets and hallways have become bedrooms, while old bathrooms, once impressively large, have been changed over and serve as kitchen *and* bathroom. Everything has been done to save space, make money, crowd people.

Through television and movies the images of these neighborhoods and apartments have become familiar. In the repetition of these images we become numb to them. We forget about the smells of the buildings, the inadequate lighting, heating, cooking facilities, the gas leaks, the hot water system that has failed or that never could supply the entire building with hot water, the added burdens caused by winter coldness, summer heat. We forget, too, about the people who are forced to live in these places.

It is also true that despite the "run-down" nature of these buildings, many tenants, on their own (for landlords and janitors typically offer little assistance), have worked to make their homes comfortable, livable, attractive. Within a single building, one may find a family living in a wholly untenantable apartment, while upstairs in the comparable apartment, a warm, pleasant residence has been created. Similarly, one finds one room well decorated, the room adjoining it in utter disrepair, just as it has been for many years.

To be familiar with America's urban centers is to be familiar with that phenomenon called urban renewal, what years ago Stokely Carmichael bitterly called "urban removal." To renew a neighborhood means to tear down the run-down structures and build bigger and, theoretically, better housing. This process in turn means moving people, sometimes into temporary housing while the new housing is constructed, but usually into their permanent home at once. These processes, too, like the sights of America's blighted areas, are familiar. Housing projects for the elderly, for example, exist in all major cities, the qualities ranging from more than acceptable to what amounts to merely another barely livable space.

The moving and reallocating of people may be taken over by agencies, special housing organizations, or it may be left to the tenants themselves. They receive their notice and make plans as best they can. Some are given ample time to arrange for their new housing, some are rushed to the extent that they cannot locate suitable accommodations, something, however unlovely, they can afford. Quite often, notice is given that tenants must leave as their building is to be torn down, but then nothing happens and they stay. Year after year the building remains, and so do the tenants.

The statistics on housing indicate that for a variety of reasons the poor move frequently. Family constellations may change, rent may be raised, a seemingly better apartment becomes available. So, with the help of friends, a move is undertaken.

Yet it is also true that despite the changing populations within communities and the consequent alterations in the physical and social character of the communities, many people wish to remain in their homes, irrespective of the condition and quality of these homes and neighborhoods. A home, after all, is real and tangible; it is a constant, a protection standing, however meekly, against the flow of time and shifts within a culture. To leave that home, in the proverbial sense, is to leave what remains of one's roots; it is to sever ties with the past and to shake the foundation of memories and prior experience. No matter how delicately, thoughtfully, skillfully, one prepares a family in the process of urban renewal—and poor families typically are not moved with especial care and caution—there is a psychological reverberation that most all people experience. Exhilarating or scary when one is young, moving often becomes a terrifying ordeal when one is older. And when one is poor, and the prospects clearly bleak, one must work hard to convince oneself that moving is not tantamount to dying.

Jacob Portman was born in Providence, Rhode Island, sometime around 1905—he has never revealed the exact date. His birth followed by three months his parents' arrival in the United States. The elder Portmans had been living in England, although their native land was Poland. Two more children would be born in America. Millie Rausch, eventually to become Mrs. Jacob Portman, was born in Romania and came to America with her parents and seven older brothers and sisters when she was eleven. She is three years younger than her husband. The Rausches settled briefly in New York, then moved to Milwaukee. Luckily, Mr. Rausch found work rather quickly, although the ensuing years would find him in and out of numerous jobs. An unskilled laborer, like Jacob Portman's father, Samuel Rausch never imagined "the American way" would be so difficult. Jacob and Millie met when they were in their early twenties. They were in New York, Millie traveling, Jacob on business. After a brief courtship, they were married in Providence, where they rented their first apartment. After several years, Jacob's business—he was a traveling salesman—took him to Boston, where the Portmans decided to establish their home. They have lived there ever since.

Jacob and Millie Portman have been friends of mine for several years. In their seventies, the Portmans, for all the time I have known them, have led a quiet life, rarely leaving their small one-bedroom apartment in a rather poor area of Boston. They used to enjoy taking walks together, but Millie's increasingly poor health has made even this activity a rare occurrence. Jacob used to like to go over to the Kuyper Home for the Elderly to play cards or visit with some friends from the neighborhood. But, as he invariably said on his return from Kuyper, the people and the building depressed him so he was happy just to stay home with Millie. At least in his house he felt safe and comfortable. At home he could be himself.

Indeed, the Portmans' cozy well-kept apartment in the

small three-story wood tenement was the center of their lives. Whatever financial and personal insecurities they might experience, they derived a feeling of strength and calm from their little home, whether sitting down together to a meal or just visiting in what they called their parlor. Whatever changes the future might bring to his wife and himself, Jacob regularly assured me, constancy and stability would be found in the apartment.

Then, without warning, the Portmans and all other residents of the small apartment house were notified that within a year the building was to be torn down in preparation for the construction of a larger apartment dwelling. The Portmans were stunned and frightened. In time, as more notices involving relocation of tenants arrived, Millie's illness seemed to grow worse, and Jacob's panic and anger increased. He wrote letters to housing authorities protesting the relocation and attended every meeting at which housing matters were to be discussed.

The following conversation, which took place during one of my many visits with the Portmans, epitomizes the concerns that so troubled the couple. Jacob and I had just returned from a meeting at Kuyper Home for the Elderly. The meeting had been scheduled so that housing officials and developers could address the people who now would be moving away from the neighborhood in which many of them, including the Portmans, had lived for thirty years. Prevented by ill health from attending, Millie had waited for us at home.

On the walk back from Kuyper, Jacob said almost nothing. Not until we had reached the apartment and he had checked to make certain that Millie was not in discomfort did he begin to speak:

"You can't describe a meeting like this today. What is it, after all? Big powers make a decision, change a neighborhood, tear down buildings. If people live in those buildings, what's the difference? They're old people or poor people. It doesn't matter, don't you see? They have power, these people, and we got—I'm not sure these days what exactly it is that we *do* have. Maybe we just have good manners; maybe that's why so many people came to that meeting. You think it's good manners?"

"I doubt it," I mumbled.

"Of course it's not. It's fright. Those are frightened people. I'll tell you something. People talk about older citizens. They speak about us like we were already dead. Or they speak about us like all we think about is we're walking around with one foot in the grave. Death, death, death. You want to know what I was thinking about there today? I was saying to myself, you know, Jacob, you're too old for this feeling, but you're afraid. Now, what the hell are you afraid about at your age? I'm over seventy years old and I'm afraid. Of what? Of *what*? Of having no place to live. Maybe I won't find a place. Or maybe they'll put us together with other people. I couldn't stand that. I'd die before that time. I need my privacy, too. I don't want other people *that* close. Like Harry Tobasch upstairs. I want him close, but not *that* close.

"You know, the poorer you get, the closer you get pushed in with people. Like today in the meeting, that was one of the messages. We're moving. That's what we're told. Not up, not down, just closer in with people. Sure, you like a little protection, but that doesn't mean you have to sleep with an army. A long time ago I settled with myself that I wasn't going anywhere in the world. I wasn't going to get a better deal; I'd probably live in this place until I died. Millie didn't care. Our child was dead, so what's the difference? That's what I used to say. So what's the difference. . . ."

I didn't hear the next few sentences. I was concentrating on the phrase "Our child was dead." In all the years I had known Jacob I had never seen a picture of a child or heard one mentioned.

"Jacob," I interrupted, "you said that—"

"That our child was dead. He was killed in Korea. He was nineteen. That's the whole story. They say Jewish boys don't fight on the street, which is a laugh. They don't fight in school, which is also a laugh. I fought. Millie's brothers fought. We all fought. A guy calls you a Heeb or steals some money, you fight. Jewish boys don't fight in wars. They get desk jobs. They're all doctors and lawyers. Another laugh. They fight, and they die. Lots of boys died. Our son died. We don't know how. A letter with no details. They sometimes send the identification tags, but his never came. I had letters from him, not many, a few. But where they are, I don't know. Somewhere they got lost. Somebody somewhere killed him, and that's that.

"I was telling you what's the difference. I was content with what would be my life," Jacob continued. His voice never quavered. "But today I know one thing: I know that I'm not going to be allowed to live like I want to, simply, humbly, however you want to call it. They're telling me, these men with power who make decisions for people like me, you, Portman, you can't stay in your home. You can't stay in your neighborhood. You can't stay with your friends. You can't shop where you always shopped, you can't walk where you always walked. And how do you like the way they're going to bus me to my *shul* if I want to go? Did you hear them talk about that? Did you see his face when he said that, trying to look like a rabbi or something? Oh, you tell me all about it you, Goy Rabbi, you. Some big shot comes to him and tells him, look, these Jews you have to address there, they're a very sensitive bunch, you know. Not like any ordinary people, sensitive. Don't make them think they're going to end up any poorer than they are, and for God sakes tell them they can keep going to their old church. They must think we're all a bunch of *chasins* or something. I can't believe this. Half the city is being bused to school, *my* generation, we're going to be bused to *shul*!

"The world is insane. There's no other word for what's happening. A twenty-five-year-old kid; you saw him. Wasn't he a kid?"

"He was young," I admitted.

"Young?" Jacob blew out a long breath. "By you he's young, by me he's a kid. Harry Tobasch leaned over to me and said, 'What is this, they don't have the decency to send a man to talk to us? They had to send a baby?' He could have been somebody's grandson. The kid stands up and he tells me, this nobody, that *I* have to get out of *my* house. This is my house, Tommy. I'm not rich. I own almost nothing; what you see in this room and in the bedroom. You want to look in the bedroom? You've been in there. Go, look, you'll see. We have nothing to hide from anybody. There's nothing I'm ashamed of. This is my home. I pay my rent and it's mine. I can read you the lease and show you. I have the right to throw people out of this house. But no more. This kid comes along and he says, *Out*! You're all moving *out*. You want to fight it? Sure, you can fight it. You can even stay in the house while they're tearing it down. What do they care? The bulldozers come and bulldoze you with the bed, with the couch, with the table and the teacups. It makes no difference to them.

"They're going to put me in a station wagon, you like that part, with a bunch of dilapidated people like me, and they're going to bus me to my new home, which is I don't even know where, and they're going to take me to my little neighborhood *shul*, let me *doven* eight times, if I do it fast, and schlepp me home again. Isn't that wonderful? Maybe they'd like to feed me while they're at it, and wash my face for me. What's going to be when it snows? I don't go to temple when it snows? You can't be a Jew when it snows around here, you know. No buses. You're Mr. Portman until November, but from December to March you're Mr. Sullivan. Did you notice how he didn't promise people housing? How careful he was with that one. He may only be a kid but he's been trained. Believe me, it shows.

"You want to know if I'm scared? I am very, very scared, Tommy. I'm not worried about dying. I'm worried about how I'm going to make out in this new plan or nonplan they've got for us. You see what that little kid did today, which maybe he doesn't even know he did? He's making me need him, *and* his organization. He's making me depend on them. And since I don't have anyone, it's got to be him. He knows it, or the big shot that taught him how to speak to us, *he* knows it. Now, every time I need something or want something, I got to depend on someone, and *I* can't live with that feeling. I could a long, long time ago, but no more. What a curse to be alive without any power at all!

"You know, I talk to you, so many things come into my mind. I feel, what's the sense of talking all the time, like I do? Then I think, but what's the sense to stay quiet? That's going to get me someplace? Then I think, what am I talking about, getting someplace, or no place? Where am I going? A person at my age, where am I going? Now comes a new thought: *They* have me thinking the way I'm thinking. These thoughts aren't coming from my heart. They're coming from the same office that boy came from this morning. The same office that tells us not only where we can't live anymore, but how to think about our lives, ourselves. Imagine that! It's fantastic really, when you think of it.

"Where am I going with my life when I'm past seventy, an old man, waiting to die? What's the difference where I live? I live here, I live there, who cares? Do *I* care? Do *you* care? Do we have any relatives, a person somewhere in the world who cares? The answer is yes, I *do* care, Millie cares, people care. Our friends care. The people at that meeting today, they weren't there only to look out for themselves. They care about other people. They care about their sisters and brothers, or their upstairs neighbor, or the people living in the building, or the people they have seder with. Huh? What about that?"

Jacob's eyes grew wide and moist. Was he thinking about the seder dinners he and Millie had attended in this room, at the Kuyper house, at friends' homes? "We care about Jews," he continued. "We care about everybody. The people in that office, though, they don't know that. To them we're just a bunch of immigrants from the neighborhood, people wheeled in, old cockers like me and Harry Tobasch, and they think, it's for this group of people we have to concentrate so much? These people take up our time, a whole one hour we have to give them on a lovely morning like this? For this group? What for? Half of them will be dead in a year. They can say whatever they want to say, I know what's crisscrossing in their mind. You know this guy Sam Milner? Used to be a tailor in New York. Family moved to Miami but his wife couldn't stand it there so they came here since she had a brother living here. Ten days after they got here the brother died. So they buried him and the whole family moved in with them. He's always been active in civic things around here. Man's a fantastic card player, too. Bridge. He was there this morning, bitching, grumbling. You think he spoke up? He fell asleep. The kid spoke ten words and Milner's sound asleep. Say bridge and he's wide awake. But move his apartment, he's asleep. I saw all this, just like the kid speaking saw it. And we're both thinking the same thing. What an audience, sleeping, dying, people can't use their muscles. How can they think we would object to anything? Put us anywhere and we'll die. Move us, don't move us, what's the difference.

"There are no long-run issues with people like us. When you're young, people say, for now, maybe, in the short run, something's not so great, but you'll put it away, like an investment, and in the *long* run you'll get dividends. You get old, there's no more long-run investments. So what's the moral? The moral is that all of a sudden, that kid this morning, he's got me convinced that what he's saying, or really what he's *not* saying because he doesn't have to say it aloud to make everyone understand it, is true. The hell with all of us. We're old, we're poor, we're Jews. It must kill people like that to even give us the time of day. I see what he sees in that Kuyper's lounge. You think any one of us would *choose* to go there? It's nothing but a place for *alta menshen* to have their wheelchairs pushed to, a place for Mr. Milner and Harry Tobasch to sleep in. You think I'm not embarrassed seeing what goes on? I'm plenty embarrassed. Milner snores, I'm embarrassed. Issac Gold stands up and gives a speech like every morning an angel comes down from heaven and tells him he's a rabbi, and I'm not embarrassed? I'd like to crawl out of there on my hands and knees.

"I'll tell you, sometimes you feel fortunate you made it to this age. But proud of it? What for? What's the achievement? The kid thinks I'm ready for the cemetery, but I don't think so. I see Milner or Gold or Bessie Klapman, I think, my God, they're old. Now *they* are *really* old. Me, I'm still a boy. In my head, I'm a boy. I still want to fight. I want to tell this kid, 'Hey, kid, I'm not an old man like I look to you. You want to know what I think, kid, about your urban renewal and your moving people around and busing me to temple which is something you don't know the first thing about? You know what, kid, you can take all your plans and stick them you know where. Go in the street and stop the first man you see and ask him, what's a *tuchas*, because Jacob Portman told me in Kuyper's funeral lounge there with the Miami hotel lighting to make it look swanky, that I should stick all my plans and promises in my *tuchas*.'

"I don't feel old, but that kid with the little planned-out speech, *he* makes me feel old. He's got me brainwashed, and that's part of his pitch. Maybe those other people understood what was happening to them, maybe they didn't. I don't know. But the message today was, move because it's natural for you to move at this time in your life. Don't look back, don't look forward either. In fact, do yourselves a great favor and don't look anywhere at all. You're a bunch of old Jews, you're lucky the city lets you stay alive. You've got no complaints, you're too old for complaints. You, Bessie Klapman, who paid for the cane you use? And you, Milner, who pays your old-age benefits so you can sleep here, or anywhere for that matter? And you, Portman, who makes it possible for you to stay alive so you can bore people out of their heads with speeches?"

"You don't bore me, Jacob," I said, uncertain whether his remark was meant for me.

"No, no," he shrugged, "a figure of speech. You know what I mean. It's the government, that's my point, it's the government that makes it possible for all of us just to survive. So what possibly can we, such dependent nobodys, have to complain about? The kid knows it, his bosses know it, the government knows it. But me, *I* want to complain. How do you like that! I want to complain. I want to stand up and make a speech so maybe God will help me a little to blow the roof off the place for me. In fact, between you and I, I'd like to blow up Kuyper's because it's a reminder of what I am, what all of us are. You see what that kid did to me today? It's all in that building. You walk into a library and everything about the place tells you, this is a place where you should be quiet and study, even if it's only a newspaper you want to read. You go to a movie picture house, no signs, no messages. But the building tells you, you come here to nosh a little popcorn and to watch a movie. That's it, nothing else. But Kuyper's, from half a block away, the building is already saying, Here, Portman, here's a place where you can come and be old and senile. Gold, you'll give a speech and embarrass yourself; Milner, you'll snore and disturb people; Klapman, you'll walk with your cane; and everybody will have cookies and orange juice and think about nothing except how old and how poor they are. It's all in the building. In the motion picture houses they used to have ushers who would show you to your seats. In Kuyper's they have invisible ushers standing around ready to show you to your grave. Look at the building, you'll see what I mean.

"You take these apartment buildings, like this one. A castle it's not. High-class it's not. But inside it's mine. I can do what I want with it. But now they're taking even that little bit

23

away from me. Tell me, is that fair? All right, I'm extreme when I talk about Kuyper's, but I don't have to go to Kuyper's. Ever. Not to watch television, not to play cards, not to see people, because if I want to see people I go to their house or they come to mine. I can buy my own orange juice. And as for those cookies they serve, *that* I need Kuyper's for? How many bakeries they got in this neighborhood? If there's one there's thirty, maybe forty. And do any of them *not* sell cookies. Big ones, small ones, brown ones, white ones. Cookies with filling, cookies without filling. You want Moses on a cookie, they'll give you Moses on a cookie. You want Jesus on a cookie, they'll give you Jesus on a cookie. But cookies at Kuyper's? They're made, I'm certain, in California and moved by truck, thirty days to get here. They've got no taste, no filling, no nothing. They're old people's cookies. They got a kid somewhere like the one who spoke this morning who they go to and they say, 'We need special cookies for a bunch of poor, old Jews.' 'What do you want in the cookies?' he asks. So they tell him what they want, and especially what they don't want, because by the time they get through telling him what's wrong with every person who goes to Kuyper's, how this one has a bad heart, and this one has a bad intestine, and this one has bad blood, and this one has no lung, what else can he put in the cookies but stones? This one can't have salt, this one can't have sugar, that one doesn't eat flour, that one gets sick from butter. See my point? I don't need them. I don't want to be reminded of what I am, or what they think I am, or what they want me to be for *their* convenience. For *my* convenience, they should leave me stay in this apartment, as lousy as it is, until I die or choose to move out. Finished. That's the end of the story. No deals, no meetings, no speeches, no cookies. If people move in who I don't like, I move. But until that time, I stay. That's all there is to it!"

One late afternoon when Jacob was out of the house running an errand, I learned that Millie was as stunned and angered by the news of having to move as her husband. In four years of visiting the Portmans, I had never heard this tone nor witnessed such energy in her:

"No peace even after seventy," she kept repeating. "Moving at fifty, sixty even, that can be done, but at seventy? What do they want from me? They couldn't let me just die on the couch, just tear down the building and bury me in the couch, on the couch, *with* the couch? And you think they'll send people over here to help us? Jacob will be pushing cartons. You'll see. He'll say no, I'm not going to, but he'll push. 'Jacob,' I'll tell him, 'on your next birthday you're going to be thirty-six years old. Should a man of that age do so much heavy lifting?' He'll say, 'Millie, are you *meshuga*? I'm over seventy. What is this nonsense about being thirty-six?' So I'll tell him, 'If I reminded you that you're going to be seventy-two, you'd be furious.' 'I don't need people to tell me how old I am. I can still count. If I want to lift cartons, I'll lift cartons.' He'd say it just that way, too. Listen, he'll have a heart attack from lifting, and when they send in some strong kid to do all the lifting, that will break his heart, too, that he's too old to do that kind of work. So how can I win? How can either of us win with this housing program they have for us?

"At this point in our lives, I think it's harder on the men. Years ago, I think I was more concerned with where we lived. Jacob had his job and I had my job, but in the house he was willing to go along with what I wanted. Now the house is all he has. With the move he began to give up. It's the first time I saw him this way. I began to give up five years ago. Five years ago, in the stretch of six months, I lost three of my closest friends. The phone rings, Esther is gone. We go to that funeral, sit shiva with the family, all of them wealthy except poor Esther. She was forgotten all her life, but she never complained. Anyway, we're recovering from that shock when it's Beverley Cohen's mother, a beautiful lady in her eighties. Thank God she died in her sleep, which is what we all pray for. You brush your hair, go to sleep, that's it. The old lady lived out her last days in a lovely house. The family has money, they didn't forget her. But she hated that place. I went once a week, religiously. I kept my promise to her daughter, but she hated the place. Such a passion, and how she talked about it. But she died, like I said, in her sleep.

"We aren't home practically from the funeral then Barbara, Beverley's daughter, dies. Out of the blue, no warning, nothing. One day fine, the next day dead. A brain hemorrhage. But from where? Not a warning. Her husband, Leonard, calls her from his office, the maid says she's asleep in the chair. Leonard says, don't disturb her, I'll be home late. That's all. She wasn't asleep. Thirty-nine years old, everything to live for. Two gorgeous children, an active husband. And not a warning. Me, I get warnings every other minute. She gets no warning and she's dead.

"It's like I tell Jacob, how bad can this move be, they gave us a very long warning. Because when there's a warning it means other people know something lousy's about to happen. So they'll try to make it better for us. And if nobody does, we'll do it ourselves. If you can breathe, you can make things better. Can you imagine how many people, and there's some in this neighborhood with the numbers tattooed on their arms, people who remember more than they want to, can you imagine them getting a notice they have to move? They're probably laughing. That's *all* the bad news? That they have to move from here to there? Like Jacob would say, 'Believe me, they're laughing.'

"It would be different if we were younger or richer," Millie continued. "The government doesn't move rich couples in their seventies, especially into some apartment house that isn't even furnished yet probably. You know these people who say, 'Millie, a million dollars here or there, it wouldn't have changed you.' Oh, no? Try me. Make *me* the experiment. I pretend I'm rich, money coming in, me giving it away, Jacob running around telling me I'm too loose with it. Whose is it, anyway? I tell him. That quiets him. I ask myself, Millie, if you had the chance to be rich or young, what would you pick? The answer is obvious, be young. Who knows, if you're young, you may have a chance to get rich. But me, I pick rich. Naturally. Youth is no guarantee of anything. Where's the guarantee? But money, *there's* a guarantee.

"Tell me, Tommy, can you imagine an old *rich* Jewish woman? Close your eyes and what do you see? The gray hair, the person hunched over a little, the mink coat, the too much makeup hiding the years that grow in the skin and stay there like little signs telling everybody this is an old lady. It's a silly sight, an old rich lady. You want to say, take off the mink and the fancy earrings, give her a simple dark dress, broken shoes, and the thick stockings, right? because an old lady has no more skin left on her legs, just veins, and mess up the hair so people think she's been working, *that's* what an old lady's supposed to look like. You try to imagine what I'm saying you'll see I'm right about this.

"Take Beverley Cohen's mother, Rosie. She felt she had dignity. That mattered a great deal to her. They put her in the home, and even with her deteriorating she had dignity. She dressed herself, or someone else dressed her, maybe her daughter arranged for all that. You pay someone and they make these old people look like movie stars. Old people are like dolls to those nurses. They play with them, dress them up, bathe them, put them to sleep. The people feel dependent on anybody, so they tell you they're like babies. I saw Rosie Cohen in that home. Every week they brought her into this room, and there she was dressed up with beautiful clothes, matching shoes, and always carrying a handbag. Can you imagine? Why all of that? Why a *handbag*? Was that the symbol of her dignity? Who knows. But I never saw her without thinking, this is a big show. She's nothing but a doll. I'm sitting here talking to a doll. But the men, no. Rosie looked foolish being rich, but the men in that house didn't. Offer me a million and I'll take it, but I still know I'd look silly being rich and old. Bad enough how I look without being rich.

"You want some advice, Tommy? Don't get old, or be poor, or tell people you're Jewish. And don't let them move you around. Stay in your house and tell anybody who wants to throw you out, wait, just wait. I'll be dead soon enough, you can have the whole damn thing then, for free. What are they going to do with all this anyway? They're going to let somebody else live here? Black people would want to come over here, what, so they can be close to the *shul*? To the kosher bakeries? Suddenly they have such a taste for matzo they're insisting they have to live here?

"What do they want to do with a bunch of old Jewish people who've never had a damn thing but wishes. Wishes. I wish I were rich. I wish this one was alive. I wish that one was dead. They can't grant us one little wish at the end of our lives? What have we done that's so bad? You know what it is? We're Jews! Nobody wants Jews near them. They get frightened. There's not that many, they think, but they're here and there, spread out on every block. Very dangerous. So let's pick them up and keep them all together. *They'll* be happier, *we'll* be happier. It's never been any different. But how do they know what I want? Do they come and *ask* me anything? They do not. They send a message I'm supposed to go four blocks away to a meeting so one of *their* representatives can *tell* me. Orders, we take orders. Is this what you win wars for, so people you never meet can send their representatives to tell you where you're going? At age seventy? No, no, no, not me. Jacob's right. I'm staying here. He won't lift cartons not because he's too old, but because *we're* too old to be forced to go through this. And I'll tell you something else. What the Jews have been through, they shouldn't ask this of us anymore. They've asked too much of us. They've always asked too much of us."

Millie Portman was alive now in a new way. She sat up

straight on the sofa, her left hand clutching a piece of tissue, her right hand on the armrest, her small thin fingers spread open. She was looking toward the window and nodding.

"How they've treated us," she resumed slowly. "Not every day, but every week. A warning, a sign, a look, a something that says, watch out. You know, people say, look at the Jews. Look how fantastic they are. So few of them, but who's like them. You hear this all the time, even from people who wish we were dead. Maybe they wouldn't go to anybody but Dr. Ginsberg but they also wish Dr. Ginsberg's mother never gave birth to him. Jews, Jews, fantastic. Jews contributing so much. But does anybody think, are these Jews happy with all they contribute? The successful ones, they don't know that people don't like them and they'll never be real members of this country, real citizens? People say, sure Dr. Ginsberg is a wonderful surgeon, but what a miserable man. Stingy, conceited, unfriendly. What's *he* got to be so miserable about with all his millions? I'll tell you what's he got to be miserable about. He knows that it's only his success that keeps him where he is. His ulcers and his headaches keep him where he is, that and his surgeon hands, or his dentist hands, or his lawyer hands. But as a man, who wants him? His hands they want, but him they have no use for. And us they couldn't care what happens to because all we're doing is using up good space and good air. At my age, they wouldn't even want my body if I donated it to a hospital. Ginsberg's hands they'll take, but my body? No, all they can do is move me to another neighborhood.

"Tell me, do I look like I belong somewhere else? Does it say on my back, 'Ship her to somewhere else?' You know what it says on my back? It says: 'A good Jew is a dead Jew.' You remember on Kuyper's wall, on the avenue side, the sign, with the swastika? Six months ago? 'A Good Jew Is a Dead Jew.' They got it off, but it goes back on. Somewhere else, maybe not the same spot, maybe not the same words, but it goes back, with the swastika.

"Or it comes in a letter that says, Move! Go—anywhere, but go! It even says please let us know if we can help. We wish you all the luck in the world. You know what that is? That's a good Jew is a dead Jew said with nice manners. Instead of drop dead, the letter says, why not move, you're only seventy-one, your whole life lies before you.

"I was going to have you investigate it for us. I told Jacob, let him look into it. *We'll* talk to a lawyer, *you'll* talk to a lawyer, we'll fight it. But Jacob's right. What for? Why all the fuss? To prove we're strong? To show the world we won't be pushed around? And why at this time in history do a bunch of sick old people suddenly have to fight? You get sick of fighting, you know that. It's just like they always say, the good fighter goes to the end fighting, but the great fighter knows when to give up. I'm giving up. Jacob's giving up. He'll drag the cartons or he won't drag the cartons. They'll tell us where to shop, we'll shop. They'll tell us where to go to temple, around here, somewhere else, we'll do what they say. We won't mess up their master plans for us.

"You know what gets me more angry than anything else? Every day I look into the mirror I see my old wrinkled *punim* and I say to myself, '*Oi*, Millie Portman, is it really you? Is it the old Millie Portman?' And I say, 'Is it *ever* the old Millie Portman.' Then I think, how come I've changed so much over seventy years that even *I* can barely recognize myself? Why is it only me? This order from the government, from people we've never even heard of, this isn't a reminder of what I've been talking about? This doesn't say it all in no words better than I could say it in a million words. You drink tea?"

"Not now," I protested mildly.

"Don't give me not now. It's not for you, the tea. *I* need to do something else but sit here and talk. Five more minutes of this and I'll be a rabbi. Tea. With milk and sugar? You want some cookies, too? *Oi*, what am I talking about cookies, I got banana cake from last night. Sylvia Mann, a doll, made banana bread and her husband brought it all the way over here on his way home from work. Wait, I'll heat it up."

"You'll join me?"

"*I*, refuse warm banana bread, with a glass of milk? What's left in the world besides warm banana bread and milk, and a *furstunken* apartment somewhere in this city which is waiting for two old Jews and their lousy few cartons? Sit still, I'll be two seconds. Time me."

Within six months of the notice of eviction, the Portmans were resettled in an apartment, of almost equal size, in a neighborhood eight miles from their old home. The three-story building in which they had spent thirty years was scheduled for demolition to make way for a twelve-story high-rise.

Given our many visits together, I was never surprised to receive a telephone call from them. Indeed, I was almost waiting by the phone on the evening before the Portmans' old apartment house was to be razed. Somehow I knew Jacob would want to visit the building one last time before the wrecking crew got to it. Sure enough, the phone call came. Jacob wondered if maybe I had a little free time in the morning, if maybe I could go with him in a sort of final pilgrimage. Of course he could understand if I was busy. I told him we would go together. As it turned out, Millie was too ill to join us.

The next morning we reached the construction site as the first workers were coming on the job. Many of them carried cups of coffee and doughnuts. They paid no attention to us, but Jacob made certain to greet practically every one of them. Then he was tugging at my arm and pulling me after him until we reached the rear of the building where we could see the back wall and windows of what was once the Portman's home.

For long minutes we just gazed up at the building, the back stairs painted gray, the drooping eaves, the green shingles, the cracking paint on the window casings. It was chilly for

Housing: Jacob and Millie Portman

May, and the sky had a peculiar silver glow. Finally, Jacob shrugged and shook his head.

"So pretty soon they bring it down. You know, I had a funny feeling everybody from the building who ever lived here would be here today. Somehow, I don't know how, they'd all find out about what's happening and be here. In fact, I saw somebody that looked like Mr. Abrams, who knows? Maybe it was. We get old—who can recognize who after all these years? But where, tell me, is that *ganif* Cranepool who was supposed to be the janitor? I say supposed to be because who could ever find him when we needed him? He's part of the story, you know. You want to know about Lester Cranepool? I'll tell you. I may be the only person who ever knew him.

"Lester Cranepool was seven hundred years old when we moved here, which was already three hundred years ago. If he was alive today, he'd be a thousand. And that's conservative!" Jacob stood in the cool morning light, his arms folded across his chest. He was smiling.

"The name Cranepool is delightful, no? But it wasn't his name. The name was Cryzanaski, pronounced like I can't say it. A refugee, a Jew, without a dime, who told the agency when he came, he needed nobody's help. If America was a free country, he'd make it with nobody's help. So that's what he did. No help, no handout, no loans, he goes looking for work. First day out he meets a man named, who knows what, who's looking for a janitor to take care of his buildings.'I'm your man,' says Cryzanaski, who's already calling himself Cranepool, which is a name he made up. 'You got a family?' the man asks. 'No.' 'You got experience as a janitor?' 'What does a janitor do?' The man tells him. 'I can do that.' 'You got the job. Twenty-five bucks a week, you work two buildings, three buildings,' what do I know. So Cranepool's the janitor. The doorknob breaks off in your hand, you call Cranepool. And I mean you give a yell, *Cranepool*!" Jacob was laughing now. The noises of the machines on the construction site began to intensify. The day was starting. The workers were preparing to begin their work. 1028 Prince Street, Jacob and Millie Portman's home for over thirty years, would be razed on this lovely morning.

"Cranepool! You'd yell, because if he had a telephone he never gave anyone the number. So you yelled, and if he was around he came. Or you put up a note for him. *Mr.* Cranepool, no less, you would write, he was a human being after all, so he got his respect, although as a janitor he was a *bum*. You think he called *me* Mr. Portman? Not once. 'What's it now, Portman?' he'd say. 'What's it now? I'll give you a what's-it-now,' I used to want to tell him. 'It's the doorknob.' 'So where is it?' 'Well, if it's not on the door it must have broken off, right?' 'So what do you want me to do?' 'Well, you got a choice, *Mr.* Cranepool.' I never talked to Mr. Cranepool; we argued, or debated, but we didn't talk. Sol Abrams, who lived downstairs, if a fly crawled on his child's nose, he brushed it off gently so he wouldn't hurt the fly. Sol Abrams hit Mr. Cranepool once he got so angry with him. 'So, Mr. Cranepool, you have a choice. Either leave the doorknob where it is and put up a whole new door, or put a new knob on the old door.' 'I'll think about it,' he'd say. 'You'll think about it? So while you're thinking, how do I open the door?' I asked him one day. 'How the hell do I open the door? I can't go in or out.' You know what he tells me? 'Go in or go out, close the door and stay there 'til I get back. What's the big decision?' 'That's wonderful, but how do I go in or go out when the doorknob's broken?' An idiot! A colossal idiot. If this man was a janitor, I'm a violin maker. 'You want to know something, Portman,' he says to me. 'More important than your doorknob is your blood pressure. Relax, I'll fix the door.' 'When?' 'When what?' 'When are you going to fix my door?' 'When I get the knob.' 'But *when*? We can't live here with the door like this.' 'So take a room in a hotel.' 'When's the door going to be fixed?' I'm so angry with this guy I could have killed him *with* the doorknob.

"I laugh about it now but when it happened, I swear to

you, I could have wrung his neck. And I knew he was a Jew. He let it be known to us. But I still could have killed him. I told the story once to the Rabbi Gitelman. He laughed and said. 'Don't kill him, you'll never get the door fixed.' 'Cranepool, when can I expect the door to be fixed?' 'What time you got?' he says to me. I look at my watch. Shmuck. Now I'm taking orders from *him*. 'It's four-thirty.' 'Four-thirty, okay, you'll have the knob on the door this century.' That's what he said. Who the hell is he, anyway? A janitor. All right, he's no worse than the rest of us, but he's no better. So I told him, 'This century? Is that a joke?' 'It's no joke,' he says. 'Listen,' I told him, 'I could rest easy if I knew for sure it *would* be this century. Knowing you, it'll be the twenty-third century.' 'So all right,' he answers. 'Then it will be the twenty-third century, and who'll be around then to care whether the door opens or not?'

"Now, while we're standing there, like you and me are doing, I learn for the first time that Cranepool is Jewish. 'What are we, anyway,' he says, 'but poor old Jews. What's the difference between a door with a knob and a door without a knob? So it locks, or it doesn't lock. Does anyone care about the door, or us? That's the important point,' he says, 'who cares about *us*? We're poor Jews, Portman,' he says. 'You with your real name, me with my made-up name.' That's when he told me his name was Cryzanaski and how he was a musician. He played the clarinet and the flute in an orchestra. When the Nazis came, they destroyed everything, and everyone he had, and he escaped, or he didn't escape, I don't know which. He has never played music since. He loved music, it was his whole life. He couldn't care less about fixing doors, or toilets, or whatever he had to do in these buildings. When the man told him what janitors have to do, he lied. He was never rich in the old country, but he never had to fix anything. His mother made sure all he had to do was play the clarinet and the flute. He hated janitor work. 'We're owned, Portman,' he told me.

'People tell me what I have to do with my hands. I used to play clarinet, now I stand here and we argue about when the doorknob gets fixed. All right, it's my job. I'll do it, but I hate it. I don't care what you think about that. It's your job to call me when things break, it's my job to fix them, but I hate it. This isn't my world, getting a handout *or* fixing doorknobs. All my life people told me how to live, *where* to live. Where's *my* freedom? After all these years, where's *my* freedom that all these people have died for. This is hell, Portman. This isn't living. This isn't a free country!'

"I didn't know what to tell him. I was still thinking about the doorknob. But he was going on and on. I didn't have the heart to stop him. But I knew, while he was talking, I'd never forget what he was saying, and that someday, I'd be telling someone about this man, because I was the only one who knew him. He lived all by himself. I went to visit him. He was always there. He was sure never in the building when the tenants wanted him. I always found him there, listening to his radio, reading the paper. He barely could read English, although he spoke it very well. From the radio, he learned, he told me. He had a little television but he never watched it, he said. Two minutes in his house, he would be giving me his speech.

"You think it's good, really, where you live, Portman?' he'd say. 'You're proud to be living there? You think it's all you deserve?' 'I don't work,' I'd tell him. 'It suits me all right.' 'What's the difference if you work or don't work? You think any person who's not in jail should live in a place like that? You think honestly *any* person should have to live in that place? You see, Portman, how you answered my question? I don't work. That's what you said. But what's that got to do with anything? You could have said, I don't deserve more because I'm a Jew.' That was true, although I shook my head. 'That's crazy.' But I *had* thought that. A Jew thinks sometimes, look, I'm alive, nobody's persecuting me, nobody's killing my wife or children, they're letting me live, what's my complaint. All right, they move you out of your apartment, but that's not killing you. I did think, like he said, a Jew gets less. He gets to live, that's all.

" 'All right, Mr. Cranepool,' I'd tell him, 'let's suppose you're right. Let's say I tell myself, I'm a Jew, I'm lucky to be in a place where they let me live. So I live in a hell, like you call it. So if I had money I wouldn't live here. So, okay, what am I supposed to do?'

"*Oi*, I can see that man's face, in his little room, not far from here on Peterborough Terrace, little basement room. I used to like going there because it was always very warm and cozy, like toast. I can see him, with the gray sweater he wore in December, in August, every day, rain or shine. '*Supposed* to do?' he says. You're *supposed* to keep on living and call me when your doorknob breaks. That's what you're *supposed* to do.' 'So why do we talk about it?' I'd ask him. 'Because if I don't talk about it, all I'll talk about is doorknobs and leaking toilets and babies messing on the stairs, and no hot water. That's why. It's my freedom, Portman; when I can think what I think when I think it. I'm not free here, Portman. Neither are you. My job tells me I'm not free, your house tells you you're not free either. We're Jews, we're poor; it all means the same to us. We don't have to define it anymore. *You* know what I mean!' Of course I knew what he meant. I've always known.

"This was two souls coming together. That's what you call it. Words take you part of the way, experience, what you've learned and felt, that's the rest of the way. He knew. I knew. 'I've always got my thoughts,' he would say. 'I always tell myself, thoughts are enough. But they aren't, I need someone to tell them to. That's why people go to temple. We go to talk, out loud, to ourselves. It's not enough just to think. So I came to your house and all I hear, from a Jew no less, is fix the doorknob. That's the biggest thing in your life? It can't be. It can't be what you're thinking about morning, noon, and night.

You must have better things going on in your mind than doorknobs.'

"I can see him in the chair talking to me. 'Tell me, Portman, tell me what you think about besides broken doorknobs.' 'I don't know,' I said. 'About being Jewish, I suppose.' 'What about it?' he asked. 'How I wish I had a better life.' I don't know, maybe I just said it to please him. Of course I thought about things, but with him I didn't know what the hell I thought about anymore. 'You think about being poor, eh?' 'Yes, I wish I had money, and a little position.' 'A nicer house, too,' he said, 'without this monster Cranepool who's never there. Go ahead, say it. It's true.' So I told him, 'All right, it's true.' 'Portman,' he says to me, and he's perfectly serious, 'you want to know what being a poor Jew means? It means when the doorknob breaks you can't fix it yourself, and you can't get anyone to fix it. A rich Jew, you know the definition? You go up to a man on the street and you say, "You know a janitor named Cranepool?" The man says, "I don't know what you're talking about." That's a rich man. When *I'm* in the picture, Portman, we're both in bad shape. I'm your reminder. When the apartment falls apart, that's a *reminder*, and when I come to fix it, *that's* also a reminder. It's also a reminder when I *don't* come. And that's when you should realize how little you have in your life.'

"I used to listen to Mr. Cranepool. Believe me. I was transfixed in his cozy little *shul* house. Each time I went there, I'd come home feeling, what a thing for a man so smart to be a janitor. At the same time, I'd ask myself, what's so special about this guy, will somebody please tell me? What has he got that I'm so afraid of, or that he makes me shy? *Me? Shy?* That's already an accomplishment. I'd think, to tell the truth, I'm not so sure I even like him all that much. First off, he tells me how bad it is in this country. It's worse than Poland? America didn't treat him good when he came? *He* was the one who refused help. America didn't give him the order: Be a janitor; you can't be a musician. And number two, where, tell me, are people free? In the Soviet Union? The Sovietskis have it all that better? When did *anyone* know freedom? So why does he bring *that* subject up? But you know what used to bother me most? I'd go and listen to him, I can't say talk because he did all the talking, then I'd leave, and the doorknob or the light switch or the toilet still wouldn't be fixed. I walk in the door and it still doesn't close right. Why should it? Talking politics with Cranepool was going to fix the door?

"So where is Cranepool now? Dead maybe. Who knows. You know, that's another reason to be rich. When you're rich, and you die, people read about it. When you're poor, people don't know. How could they? So where's Cranepool? Where's all my friends? Where are the people from this building? Where's the door, with or without the knob? Can anybody tell me that: Where is the door?"

Jacob straightened up and looked one last time toward the old building. He adjusted the collar of his suit jacket and let out a long breath. "*Nu*, that's it. My speech, my visit. The main thing is that we came. It's like people say when they come out of temple, '*Oi*, was the rabbi in good form. *Oi*, was the rabbi in bad form.' What's the difference, I always tell them, at least we came. That's the important thing. Today you and me, we were here, so thank you, now we'll go. If you could give me a lift to the 196 bus, I can make it. . . ."

"Jacob, I'll drive you home."

"It's out of your way."

"What are you talking about? It's near my home. It's right where I'm going."

"You're not lying?"

I grinned at him. "You're a pest, Jacob."

"This I knew before this morning."

We tramped out of the demolition site, slipping, it seemed, on the same rocks and rotten timbers we had slipped on when we entered the yard. This time Jacob didn't take my hand. At first he walked with his hands pushed deep inside his jacket pockets, but soon he had freed them to keep his balance.

What he said filled my mind. Would I be able to remember it? How could I connect all the pieces of his recollections? Would it be melodramatic to try to locate this Mr. Cranepool, and would Jacob like to meet the man again? But wouldn't it be marvelous to walk to the front of the building and find a man peering up at the windows only to have him turn out to be Lester Cranepool? The two men would recognize each other and embrace, perhaps even weep. But if not Mr. Cranepool, then at least one other old tenant should be there, paying his last respects to the building.

Reaching the sidewalk, we stamped the mud off our feet and walked around to the front of the building. No one was there. Jacob spent only a second glancing toward the front entrance, but he never broke stride. We continued to the end of the street and turned the corner. Throughout the walk we continually looked behind us catching sight of the building. From the street running parallel to Prince Street, we saw the rear of the building, the part where we had stood and talked. Then it disappeared again, until we reached my car. One final look from both of us and we got in. As I started the motor, I heard Jacob whisper, "So, that's it."

We drove off, passing still again in front of the building. Turning right at the same corner where moments before we had walked, I proceeded slowly, believing that Jacob cherished every second, but his eyes were fixed on the sidewalk.

"That's it," he whispered again.

Suddenly I felt Jacob's hand on my arm. It was a forceful gesture that pulled the car to the right.

"What's wrong, Jacob?"

"That woman walking there."

I slowed down. A car behind us honked. "You know her?"

"Of course." He was grinning broadly at the sight of the

woman approaching us. She was walking in the direction of Prince Street.

"Who is it?"

"Mrs. Abrams. From the building," he said softly.

"You want me to go back?" The woman had already passed us as I pulled the car over to the curb.

"What are you stopping for?" Jacob grabbed my right wrist and pushed it up, forcing the car back into the street. "Don't stop!"

"You don't want to talk to her? How long has it been since you've seen her?"

"Fifteen years, maybe. I don't even know for sure."

"Didn't you want to talk to her?"

"About what?" he asked. He turned to look at me with a lovely smile. His face showed the strains of the morning. He began patting my hand. "We both know where she's going, and why she's going there. You see that, she knew. We don't have anything to talk about this morning. Another day, yes, but this morning we leave each other alone. You see how it is? She makes her visit, I make my visit. You see that? You didn't believe me when I told you a place like where tomorrow is going to be rubble could be sacred. A place can be like a cemetery without the bodies six feet under. You didn't believe me. Maybe Mr. Cranepool was right, maybe he wasn't. You see how it is?" Jacob's blue eyes shone brilliantly, and he was nodding emphatically. "He may have been wrong in the end, that Cranepool. How do you like that! You didn't believe the old man, huh?"

"I believed," I said.

"Good for you," he said, still patting my hand and looking straight ahead at the road. "Good for you. *Mazel tov*," he whispered.

"*Mazel tov*, Jacob."

Two

Kinship and Friendship: Ella Crown

In my work with the people introduced in these pages, themes of kinship and friendship constantly recur. The interconnection of human beings, their bonds, their ties by blood, friendship, marriage, or through mere acquaintanceship is in large measure the glue that binds the individual to his or her history, community, neighborhood, and the larger social order.

Every time I left the homes of elderly people like Jacob and Millie Portman and especially Ella Crown, whose words appear in this chapter, I felt their solitude. Who talks with them? I wondered. Who knocks on their door? Who stops them on the street to gab a little, to have a *schmooz*? Who telephones at night to ask about them or establish from the tone of their voice if they are well? If they needed something, whom would they call? Whom would they dare to disturb?

Millie Portman once told me. "The secret of life is to have one good friend. If it's your husband or wife, then God has really shown his face. But you need one person who you can nudge to death and they won't leave you." Like Millie, the others I worked with gave continual evidence of their need for human attachments. In some cases the bond could be to anyone, simply having a friend. In others the need was to be close to their nearest kin.

Bonds of friendship are intense and nothing short of life-giving. As we all know, severing them can cause great pain and harm. But kinship carries an extra energy and power, and an extra burden, too. When shattered, such bonds leave an emptiness like death. Equally, when kinship bonds take on the bland, innocuous quality that they will from time to time, this, too, can evoke feelings of demise and decimation. In fact, the empty bond of kinship, the bond that exists in name alone, may be the most dehumanizing and ultimately destructive form of separation family members experience.

"At least if your kid stays angry," Ella Crown told me once, "you know he's still there. It's when they stop calling that the fire goes out."

Ella Crown, born Eleanor Rachel Sapolsky, does not remember anything of the first years of her life in Poland. She has vague memories of her family's migration to America; she believes they lived in Holland for several months waiting for passage, but then again, it may have been Belgium or even northern France. The middle of five children, one of her sisters died on the boat coming to America. Another child died soon after the family arrived in Baltimore, where her family lived for several years before moving to New York. When Ella was twenty-two, she married Ben Crown, a man who looked to all the Sapolskys as someone with a promising future because he had a keen mind for business. Ben Crown was born in America, which made him special in the eyes of the Sapolsky family, although Ella found him special for other reasons.

After more than forty years of marriage, Ben died, leaving Ella to live very much alone, as by then her parents and all remaining siblings had also died. The Crowns had one child, a daughter.

Ella Crown was convinced she would never outlive her husband, Ben. Now in her middle seventies, she has not known good health for many years. She has several close friends, but since Ben's death over a decade ago she prefers to spend the majority of her hours by herself. By her own admission a fussy woman, she likes to keep things exactly as she wants them. She is disturbed by people who tell her how to lead her life, arrange her furniture, save her money. She knows her situation better than anyone, she tells friends. If all they have for her is suggestions, they would do better staying away.

Behind Ella's pleasant appearance is an anger that has increased over the last ten years. She cannot rely on anyone, even though she dreads the idea of depending upon people for the slightest thing. It's bad enough, she says, collecting welfare checks and feeling embarrassed over the fact that you're depending on other people's money to keep you alive. Yet what has troubled her the most is the realization that no one depends on *her*. Her comings and goings affect no one in the world, just as her death would matter only slightly to the few relatives with whom she barely keeps in contact.

Ella Crown lives in a two-room apartment in Boston. One room has an electric heater, the other is usable only in the warmer months. As her building was originally converted from what was once a mansion, several unusual features have been retained. For one thing, the bathroom is so large it is used as kitchen as well. A small refrigerator stands alongside the wooden-seat toilet. An electric stove has been placed next to the sink. On cold days the stove makes the room bearably warm, even though using it as a radiator causes Ella's electric bill to skyrocket. The kitchen-bathroom arrangement breaks innumerable housing and fire code regulations, but nothing has been changed since the problem was first reported seven years ago. Another old feature of the building is a huge floor-to-ceiling window that looks out over a tiny courtyard near the corner. Unfortunately, the window is in the unheated room, which stays closed during the winter. Ella puts rags and towels in the loosely fitting door so that the cold will not get into the apartment.

Often when I visit her, as I have for several years now, she will be baking. Her hands are thin-skinned, but the fingers work easily. Her eyesight, however, has decreased significantly. She complains constantly about her glasses. Perhaps the prescription is not correct, perhaps some of her older glasses would be better now, perhaps she would do better wearing no glasses. "*Oi*," she mumbles, studying the apple cake ready to go into the oven, "you get old and the machinery doesn't work anymore. Point to a spot, I'll show you a pain. Ach, it could be worse. How, I don't know, but I heard someone say that once, so *I* keep saying it, too. Oh my God." Ella straightens up and puts her hands on the lower part of her back. "I think I left the vanilla *and* the sugar out. You like vanilla?"

"I can take it or leave it," I answer.

"I hope the cake feels like you do." Bending over as if she were a mother kissing a sleeping baby, she speaks to the cake: "Please don't hate me, but I think I left out the vanilla." She picks up the cake and turns it toward me for one last look. "*Nu*, say a little *barucha*, please, for the cake."

Ella leans over and slides the cake into the oven. Then, pushing back her glasses, she attempts to focus on a clock mounted high on the wall. "What's the difference what the time is. We'll come back and check up in a little while." One last turn toward the stove and a finger comes up, pointing menacingly toward the cake: "Call if you get burned." Then she looks at me. Her expression says: What harm can it do talking to a cake?

At last we are sitting in the apartment's one barely warm room, both of us bundled up in sweaters. Ella and I have had several conversations about this room. Inevitably these conversations turn to her health and well-being. It isn't good for her to be in a place like this, I say. It isn't wise for her to be living alone anywhere, especially in a firetrap. But she likes it here; it is her home. Besides she has said, "What's to worry about now? At the end of a person's life somebody discovers the way they're living isn't ideal. So? And besides the besides, it's people living with people, treating one another in decent ways that matters, not where you live, or how you live, or with who you live. People worry about whether rooms are too cold or toilets are kitchens or kitchens are toilets. I'm all right. I've got people I could scream to. They'd come and bring me anything I need. Believe me, I'll call plenty loud if I need something."

Ella Crown lives with a flood of resentments. They don't show at first meeting, but in time they reveal themselves in the endless comparisons she makes with people she claims have "come through life" better than she has. A contemporary, Rosalyn Silverstein, is one of these people:

"Is that a great woman, that she can walk with her nose in the air? That she can come into your house and criticize? That she can tell you, you don't have to dress like you're really the age you are? Did her husband do anything with his life? Did he make so much money? Did he put her in a great big house that people went weak when they saw it? What's so special about her that gives her the right to tell people what to do with their lives? And how come of all the people in the world, *her* daughter has to marry a rich man with a clothing store? Every week she gets clothes, new fashions, old fashions. What did she do to deserve it? Did she take such wonderful care of her child? She played cards more than she spent time with her child, now she gets new dresses.

"All right, so here's a case of God being good to someone. With all the sadness in the world, it's nice to have a little *mazel* fall on someone you like. But I don't need this woman coming into my house and telling me she's going to get me dressed up at her son-in-law's place. If I want to go to her son-in-law's place I'll go on my own two feet. What is she, some social worker that

45

she's going to dress me up like a doll? I don't want handouts. Welfare, Social Security, Medicare, I've got that coming. But handouts I don't want any part of, especially from people who haven't worked a day in their lives. Whose money is she giving away so freely after all, not hers! She's embarrassed that I'm here and she's wherever she is, which I don't even know because I won't go to her. I'm stubborn, I'm an old lady, but a few things I can still do on my own and one of them is stay at home when I want to and see the people *I* want to see, and dress the way *I* want to. You see my clothes, are they so dirty, ripped? I look like what I am. I'm not rich, what should I have a costume for. You don't need friends like Mrs. Silverstein, the dress store mother-in-law. If her son-in-law wants to go 'round bragging how he takes such good care of her, fine! Let them name him Man of the Year and his mother-in-law Woman of the Year. I don't love what I have, but it's honest goods. *She* can't say that!"

Ella's voice gets stronger as she speaks, her way more assured. Yet she has told me on many occasions that at her age it makes no sense to wonder how things might have been. "That's for people approaching the latter years, not for people smack in the middle of the end.

"People who wonder how it might have been, they're beginning to see the years slip away. They still have opportunities left, but they see how the opportunities get fewer and fewer. Still, there's always a bit of time left for them to make a change here, a change there. At my age, you don't wonder about the might-have-beens. They say old people do nothing but think about the past. How much future, after all, is there? But think only about my memories? That's crazy. Maybe when you're lying in a hospital ready to die that's all you think about, but that isn't me.

"Any might-have-beens I think of now don't relate to the past; they relate to right now, today, maybe as far back as yesterday. It might have been nice someone could have come over yesterday like they promised. It might have been nice if

46

they couldn't come, they could have sent a message. That's the kind of thing that might have been nice. But might-have-beens in my entire life? I can't think that way. You take what life has to offer and stop punishing yourself. After a while, every person has to realize they got a little bit of war going with their parents, their children, and themselves. Even at my age it happens. No one has it all good with their families, even after your parents are dead *decades*, and your children are so old they don't need you anymore. Need you? They don't *want* you, not even to baby-sit or bake a little something. My mother's dead fifty years and I'm still angry with her. Why am I angry? I'm angry because she didn't take me to plays or concerts when I was small. She didn't buy me nice clothes. All my life I got hand-me-downs. That's why I'm angry with her. Because I liked some kind of pudding or cookie, who can remember now, and we didn't have them often enough. And tell me, if we had what I wanted six days a week would I not be angry with her for not having them the seventh day? A child is angry, but here I am, at my age, and I *still* remember all this. Even while I'm laughing, and maybe feeling a little sad with all these memories, I'm still angry with her. I'll go to my grave fighting all the little wars. If I had a wish for my own daughter, I'd tell her, don't fight the little wars. Let them all go. You got a right to be angry but don't hang on. People hang on to things, to people, whatever is there. I hang on to this place. Why not? If they make a law I can't hang, I'll let go. Not because I'm drowning, but what else have I got?

"You want to know why I'm still angry with my parents? Because they never educated me properly. They knew what was right, and they had enough of the right things around. They pushed with the religion, but where was the rest of it? They *should* have pushed. Other families pushed. All right, they had no money, but I could have done plenty of things all the same. I was the only child. Two babies died. My mother never got over it, I suppose. In my way, I had to be such a grown-up, and so soon, I never bothered to ask her about it. But where were the chances for me? They showed me nothing of the world. We never traveled, we never went shopping, for penny candies even. We used to go on a streetcar, that was supposed to be the big adventure of the month, but she hated the streetcar, going places. So with all her hating, she made me hate it, too. I made the same mistakes with my own daughter, but at least I exposed her to things.

"You know what I wish? I wish I could play the piano. Upstairs, there's a family. Petrovsky. They don't have money but they got a piano. I think, how I'd love to be able to play the piano. What a feeling. I used to know a little. I knew from the black notes and the white notes. Isn't that a shame? My mother could have arranged for piano lessons. What did it cost? What a gift to give to your children, music, dancing, painting. Even cooking. You think she gave me cooking lessons? Not one. I watched her, I learned a little. But why didn't she do that? And tell me this, after seventy years of thinking about all this, why am I still fighting all these battles? Why am I still in the Spanish-American War? At least I should be in World War I. It's time for that, no?"

Ella and I sit next to one another on the beige couch. The old wooden floor is stained dark brown. It is sorely scratched but it retains a warm feeling. The high ceiling is gray with dirt, and cracked; some of the pieces hang down like bat wings. Ella and I have spoken of the disgraceful condition of the building, her two rooms in particular. She has told me how she imagined it looked when it was in what she calls its heyday, and how it actually looked when she moved in shortly after Ben died. A prostitute named Mandy had been living in the apartment. There was not much of a kitchen, but the condition of the rooms was better than it is now. Mandy had used the front room with the tall windows as a waiting room. A few chairs were placed in the waiting room, a bed, dresser, and small dressing table in the back room. Thin shades covered the windows.

The people who lived upstairs in those days, before the Petrovskys and Frenches moved in, remembered Mandy as a model tenant. She made no trouble and went out of her way to be pleasant. The only uneasy moments came when rich clients visited her. They looked out of place, these well-to-do men with their long handsome overcoats and shiny shoes. Some of them came to know the tenants by name. They claimed they were doctors on house calls, personal friends, insurance men, but everyone knew their business. The men lied, partly to protect themselves, partly to honor the tenants, and especially Mandy herself.

When Ella first moved into the apartment, the men visitors continued to call. Ella laughed at their surprised and embarrassed expressions. "I can't help you, can I?" she teased them. Confused or openly horrified, the men would quickly disappear into the darkened stairwell. But one, a man named Theodore Gheeley, once stayed to speak with her and explain why, as an attractive businessman in his mid-thirties, he had sought out a prostitute. He spoke with Ella of his loneliness, the ambition of his wife for social standing, and his sadness that she could never understand his own modest ambitions. That is why he enjoyed seeing Mandy. She understood men and their loneliness in marriage. "And what, she didn't please you also on the side, and on the front and back, too?" Ella quipped, perplexed suddenly by the problems of the rich. "Maybe you loved her. Or she loved you." Mr. Gheeley had pondered the idea. "I love the idea of loving someone," Mr. Gheeley had mused. "It hasn't happened, and all the money won't make it happen." "You won't make a deal?" Ella inquired. "My loving for your money?" Mr. Gheeley did not respond. "Loving I've known," she continued, "money I haven't. I'm ready now to make some trades."

Before he left, Theodore Gheeley offered to pay Ella's rent. "Send me the bills," he had said. "You can tell people I'm a relative if it bothers you." "If I let you pay the rent," she had responded, "I'd tell people you're my lover." He kissed her lightly on the cheek and told her that if he located Mandy, he would send her to visit Ella. "Look at this," Ella remembers saying, "I'm in a new place three weeks and already I'm tied in with the underground." Theodore Gheeley laughed. "The aboveground should be so good," he whispered, heading for the stairs. "What kind of a name is Gheeley?" she called after him. "A sad name" came the reply from the darkness.

Ed French, the man who lived upstairs of Ella, had told her that Mandy was a Negro. "You talk to her?" Ella wondered. "Never," he said. "But she *was* a Negro. You could tell." "You usually can," Ella told him calmly. So, she had thought, she was now a welfare widow, living in rooms once occupied by a prostitute, who was also a Negro. Moreover, she had already met several of the old clients. In fact, Theodore Gheeley was intent on making friends with Ella. He sent her flowers twice a month. A Negro prostitute and a rich businessman, Ella would think. Maybe there's a point to all of this thing called the rest of my life.

Then one day came a knock on the door, and before her stood a tall, thin, dark-skinned woman with black eyes, full lips, and a bright orange scarf wrapped around her head. Ella looked surprised. "Could it be Mandy?" "It could be," the young woman answered. "Mr. Gheeley," Ella grinned. "He's making his arrangements again, eh? Or did you leave something behind?" "I came to see *you*," Mandy said.

Ella's face lights up as she tells me about her meetings with Mandy: "You want to know about Mandy? Well, to begin, she *did* love Mr. Gheeley, my secret mystery lover. I never let him pay my rent, of course, but he would have. I didn't want his pity, I couldn't stand that, but I liked him. Our backgrounds couldn't have been more different, but maybe it was because we were both so lonely in those days. It's over for him. He died. I never wrote him. He died of cancer. Mandy told me. She refused his money, too. She wouldn't sell him love. But she loved him. And he loved her. He was hurt and sad and lonely, but he knew enough to know what love wasn't and what it was.

"*Oi*, there's so much I could tell you about Mandy, and one thing I'd love to tell Ed French. Mandy a Negro? She wasn't any more a Negro than I am. She was born Sophia, a Moroccan Jew whose mother was Egyptian. Her father died, her mother went to Israel, she came here as a child to live with an aunt. She wanted to be a beauty parlor owner and thought maybe she'd go to Israel. She needed money, so this is what she did, and here's where she did it. Theodore Gheeley knew all about it. He knew we were both Jews. With my face, there's no disguise. Sophia, she could be anything. She isn't gorgeous, but she's got a good heart. What, she's had it easy? Nobody who comes to this building has it easy.

"But you know, when she first told me, I thought, My God, what is happening to me? I've got a social worker who comes and asks questions about my personality and *I'm* talking to prostitutes. Then I thought, I'm not proud of her. There are ways to make money when you're young. Here's an attractive woman who speaks maybe three languages, what's she doing all this for? When I first found out, I got a boy in here and paid him a few dollars to clean the place up all over again. You think that's a normal mind working? What's the boy going to wash away, the memories? My fears? Her shame? She didn't have shame. She talked to me about her business like Mr. Gheeley talked about his business. I go around being a prostitute, and what do you do? *Nu,* I told her, I'm a professional widow. She laughed at first, but then she saw my meaning. Still, a woman has no money, she has no parents around, this job pays more for less time working, so you do it. What, she should take in washing and ironing like we used to do forty years ago? She had a doctor as a client, he examined her regularly, he took care of her teeth, what's the fuss. I told myself, Ella, you're old; in the body a lot, in the brain worse. This woman who chooses to call herself Mandy and maybe even makes herself look like a Negro because she's maybe ashamed that as a Jew in America she's reduced to this, wants to make a living, who the hell am I to criticize? How, tell me, do I question *that* but not a bathroom which is also a kitchen?

"People tell me I shouldn't live like this. You think people *choose* to live like this? You do what you can, with your body, your hands, your *tuchas*, anything you've got. I learned my lesson too late. I had to get old to learn it. I had to have a husband die before I learned it. Here's a woman, nineteen years old, *she* learned it. She found out how the world runs, I pretended like I didn't. So I don't question. And from all of that, I got a friend who comes and brings me what I need, what I don't need, but what she *wants* to bring me because she enjoys it. What is she, my daughter? She comes Tuesday morning, Thursday afternoon. I'm making dinner, in she comes. Does she let me know? Never, But there she is, six o'clock, all made up with the fancy jewelry. What's she want? She's going to a store, what do I need? She's got a shopping bag and she's keeping a place in it to buy for me. And take money from me? As a last dying wish I could offer her money and she wouldn't take it. So she goes out and she buys for me. Soap, paper napkins, soup, bread, a little this that's on sale, some towels for the kitchen.

"One night she comes in all excited. She has a radio for me. Where'd you get it? I asked. How could I take it? Green stamps! She saved up from green stamps and got me a radio. Ten at night she comes in with a friend of hers, and this one's a *real* Negro. No Moroccan Jew this one, and the three of us listened to the basketball game. They told me they couldn't stay because they were going to a party. They couldn't stay but they stayed for two hours. I whispered to Mandy, 'He knows what you are?' 'The whole world knows,' she said. 'The whole world knows?' Not Ed French, that blind *mamzer*. But Ed French, he never knew because he was ashamed of what he was. He didn't talk to anybody because he thought if you talked to somebody they'll find out you don't have much money. All he had to do was once in his life talk to the Petrovskys, he would have found out. Two years Mandy lived here she spent every holy day with them. Passover, Yom Kippur, a couple of days of Hanukkah. You know why I'm angry at him that he never bothered to find out? Because you must find out about people, otherwise you're dead. You must start to think thoughts of other people, otherwise you're alone, like Ed French. And I'm angry because that's me, too. *I'm* the one who sees somebody passing by and already, without saying a word, I have ideas about them. That means people think this way about me. She's old, and she's a widow, she lives on welfare, she's *Jewish*, so that means she must be this and that.

"So how will we ever learn about each other? French, he's ashamed of being poor. The Petrovskys, who knows about them? And do I not have my prejudices? How could she be a prostitute? How could a married man come to see her? She doesn't know sadness? Behind all the smiling and the laughing and the jewelry and the happy going shopping at nights for radios, there isn't sadness? People see me, they say, she must be so bad off, poor thing. Let's get her flowers, or a radio. But I'm not so bad off. I have people come to see me, they find me entertaining. Did poor Theodore Gheeley have to *buy* that from her in the beginning. He paid for *everything* in the beginning. I paid for nothing. It all came with the apartment. See what I mean? Like they used to say, courtesy of the management."

The apple cake was finished. The smells coming from the kitchen were enticing. Ella knew she had made something special. "A good cook," she said softly, "can work in any kitchen, and this, believe me, is any kitchen." Then we were back in the main room, eating cake and sipping milk from little glasses with strawberries on them. Ella always shrugged off my compliments. "What does it take to follow a recipe? Anyway, you're too easy to please. But maybe better easy to please than hard to please, like someone else I know."

The bitterness about her daughter and son-in-law never subsided. That there was never enough time for her daughter to visit deeply pained Ella. "How is it possible," she would say, "that people of the same blood can't find the time when people of different blood can? The wars still have to keep going?" Wars or not, Marilyn Kahne didn't have the time, or the inclination, to meet with her mother more than once a month. When I asked about it, Ella would say, "Busy she isn't, famous she isn't, old she isn't. But impolite, disrespectful, *that* she is!" Many of our conversations contained no reference to Marilyn, but on this one day, Ella spoke of her daughter, and with anger. Ella had just celebrated a birthday. Marilyn had sent a card with a ten-dollar bill tucked inside, but there had been no visit.

Ella put her plate down and drank the last bit of milk in her glass: "I should excuse it, but I'm sorry I can't. I can't let these things happen and pass them off. My daughter was very involved with her father, like a lot of daughters. His death was hard on her. They had a little something between them like a lot of fathers and daughters. I wasn't left out, but she was never the same with me. Now it's ten years since he died, so how long does it have to be before we can get a little closer? She resents me, maybe, for his dying? I didn't take good enough care of him in her eyes? Maybe she thinks I wasn't the world's greatest wife or housekeeper. Children judge you, you know. All the time, they're looking at you and judging. But once in her life, do you think she ever judged her father? Oh, no, you don't do that, because I'm the one didn't meet her idea of what a good wife is. But does *he* get blamed for barely earning enough money or having no good insurance? Does he get any of the blame for us living in those dreary places we lived in all our lives, apartment hotels? No, why should she blame *him*? He played little games with her and they went on walks and had their secret adventures. He was perfect. *I* was the one who was making us poor, because I did the shopping and the cooking and cleaning. She didn't like the food I made, or how I kept house; she didn't like the clothes we got her, so it was *me*! So now she's getting even with me. Here's a woman almost forty, and she thinks like a girl no more than five. Blame the mother. That's all they know.

"But does anyone want to know how *I* think about it, how *I* hated living where we lived? We never even had a dream. There was never any talk of *someday* we'll have money and we'll move and travel. It was always, how much do we have left? They're cutting back on overtime pay; the insurance benefits are going down, the prices are going up; we have to begin to do without. That was his famous expression: 'Ella, you'll have to learn to do without.' Without? Who had *with* all those years? We were crippled by a shortage of money that started when we were children and keeps going to this day. And what, my daughter married such a rich man? They're just keeping their heads above water. They don't like to admit it any more than we did, but it's like trying to make people think you don't have a nose on your face. You don't hide what's right there in front of everyone.

"So there she is in her little apartment, the grand total of thirty minutes away by bus, because her rich husband just sold his car, but she's going to carry on the pretending that it's different now. That girl was very well taken care of when she was a child. I'll tell you something, we *did* hide our situation in those days. She went to school, had new shoes, new clothes, she never went hungry, people didn't know what our situation was. They needed costumes for plays, what, I told her her father doesn't earn enough money for food so how do you expect to have a costume you'll wear once? Tell me the costume, we'll get you the costume. A fairy, a queen, a prince, come on, we'll measure you, we'll make it. Somehow we'll get a costume.

"We asked no one at any time for a loan. Learn to do without, she didn't hear the words. Mother, this year the children wear black boots, not white boots. Okay, we go get black boots, like we had money to burn, huh? But for the daughter, you do everything for the daughter. My husband and I lived in an apartment smaller than this. One bedroom, a living room, and a kitchen. And who slept in the bedroom? Did we? No, she did. In the living room inside a closet was a fold-down bed, *that's* where we slept. Every morning up goes the bed, every night, down comes the bed. That makes us rich? *She* had a bed, with a cover on it that *she* picked out, and the dolls and the stuffed animals. We had two worlds in that apartment hotel, her world and our world, and *I* was the reason our world looked so bad. A girl friend comes over after school, and *she's* embarrassed because I didn't push our bed up inside the closet. You know what my daughter wants, she wants her friends to think we sleep in a bedroom somewhere else, or maybe we rent the whole floor.

"All right, she's ashamed, but how long is this supposed to go on? I'm living in such great wealth now, she thinks when he died I took all the money and gave her nothing? I *wish* that was the case. If I had money it *wouldn't* go to her and that husband of hers who's always got such a wonderful deal he's cooking up. So Martin, how's the business? Around the corner, Ella. We're so close you can almost see it. They must think people like us are really dumb, or we're blind and deaf. Why can't they give up the pretending and say look, we're getting along, not as good as we want, but we're also not in the gutter. No, they have to pretend. Her father didn't pretend with me, but he taught *her* how to pretend, so now she taught her husband the same game.

"Someone comes and gives us money, I'd give it to her, but I'd make her promise the pretending's over. I'd love to give to my Mandy, but she's going to be all right without all of us because she uses her head. But my daughter, all she uses her brain for is pretending. She wanted a family, that's fine. But when do you get old enough that you face up to what you don't have and what you'll never have. You want another piece of cake?"

Ella's hands had begun to shake. She tried to keep from

looking at me. She rose and went into the kitchen, where she pretended to work, but I could see her rearranging pots and pans.

"Ella, let's sit down, we'll talk about something else," I proposed, bringing my dirty dishes into the kitchen. "I'll wash up."

"Don't wash up." She pushed me away. "Now, look," she began forcefully, "I know you talk to me for your work. But you talk to me as a friend, too. I tell you things that matter to me. I'm not going on forever, neither is my daughter. There has to be a change, and it has to come soon. The pretending doesn't go on without a big price being paid. It's already taken one person from this family. I said he didn't pretend but maybe he did. Maybe she would have thought better of me if once I had said, all right, we're stopping the pretending. Maybe if I'd done that I'd have set a pattern she could have followed. But now it's too late for that. Now the pretending gets in the way of her seeing that she also disliked her father because he pretended. She hid behind all the pretending, and she's still hiding. She can't tell anybody how angry she is, so she takes it out on me. But she's still angry with her father.

"Maybe all the costumes and the white boots and the black boots and her having her own room when her parents didn't have their room was the pretending that's made her unhappy. Maybe she was ashamed for getting the little bit extra that we could give in those days. Maybe the big mistake was not saying, look, Marilyn, we love no one more than you, but *you* sleep in the fold-down bed. A bedroom is for parents, and when you get older you'll find out why it has to be that way. Who knows, maybe that was the real mistake. And for *that* I blame me. *Oi*, so now that that's off my chest, where's the man with the million dollars? Isn't that supposed to be what happens? You put your finger on the truth and the door flies open and there's a man with a million dollars? So who's the man? Theodore Gheeley? *You*, I can see," she said with a large grin, "don't have a million dollars. But tell me, if you don't come from the kind of home I'm talking about, can you understand anything I'm saying?"

"I understand some of it, Ella," I replied.

"If a person is human, he can understand what this is all about. Everybody knows what goes on in families, but I always say, there's always one more thing in the family besides the people, it's the honesty between the people. Money doesn't make it easier to be honest. Did Mr. Gheeley have to be poor? He couldn't be honest? Ben's gone, and I still have a daughter, thirty minutes from here. All right, she sent a card for my birthday, I appreciate that. But visiting is what matters, and more than visiting, I need honesty; I want it from her, I want it *for* her. This I *know* you understand. A little more cake?"

I shook my head.

Ella leaned on the counter and gazed at me intently. "Do you know my daughter and me can't *look* at each other; can you think of something sadder than that? Do I even know if it would have been better if we had money in those days, if we had real beds in bedrooms, like you're supposed to have? Come into my bedroom." Ella winked at me, and we walked back into the bedroom-sitting room. "Sit on the bed," she ordered gently. I obeyed. "It's comfortable, no?"

"Terrific," I said, feeling embarrassed.

"Go ahead, put your feet up."

"I've got shoes on, Ella."

"I can see you have shoes on. Go ahead, put your feet up, lie down. You don't eat my cake, now you won't put your feet up."

I lay my head on the pillow and stretched out.

"Now close your eyes."

My God, I thought, what possibly could be coming next?

Ella giggled. "You're a little nervous, aren't you? Tell the truth, even with me, an *alta madel,* you're sweating. Look on your lip and see how you're sweating. We're not going to make love, if that's what you think."

"I didn't really . . ."

"You were thinking that, a little. You go looking to write a book and you end up with an old lady who's complaining because her daughter won't visit her. Don't worry, we can't make love because the welfare system says I'm not supposed to."

I could barely speak. My eyes were closed, my body so tense I could feel pain in the muscles of my back and shoulders. The teasing was not uncharacteristic of Ella, nor were the anger and defiance. She reminded me of the child who wants to let others know that she can be tough so that they will not see her vulnerabilities.

"Now, get the feeling of it," she was saying. "That's *my* bed. Nobody takes it from me. I don't shove it into a closet during the day. I don't have to feel ashamed if it's unmade. I don't have to feel *anything* if I die in it, tonight, or any night. Tell me this," she went on almost triumphantly, "tell me whether just lying there, you can be sure you're rich or poor?"

"I can't tell."

"You could be anything, right?"

"From where I'm lying, Ella, I could pretend anything."

"That's the point. So tell me, why at my age do I still pretend? Why does Marilyn pretend but not Mandy, who you would think has so much to hide? I could cry, except I'm too old. I'm an old lady with a very unhappy daughter. *Nu*, I told another big truthful thing, so *now* where's the knock on the door and the man with a million dollars? How many truthful things does an old lady have to tell before the knock comes? You're comfortable on the bed? Take your shoes off."

"I'll have to be going soon."

"I'm keeping you. I'll tell you, today I told so much truth I'm really expecting a wonderful thing to happen. And I'll tell you one thing more. I pretend I'm better off by myself but I'd like things different between my daughter and me. Everybody's walking around with a smile, but in the heart, where nobody else can see, there's an ache. It doesn't get any easier when you get older. More and more of you aches. The body gets smaller, the ache gets bigger. Marilyn, poor thing, she's going to find out the hard way. But I think my friend Marilyn knows about it already. Go! It's late. Here, take some cake with you."

I put on my coat as Ella returned to the kitchen to tinker with pots and pans. Again she refused my offer to help clean up.

When we made our arrangements to meet again, she said, as she always did, "Don't come if you feel sorry. Do it for your work."

As I moved toward the door she continued:

"Don't catch cold out there and don't bring presents when you come."

"Then don't make cakes for me."

"Who are you," she protested, "telling an old lady what to do? If I want to bake, I'll bake. You don't let me bake, you don't let me live free. You believe that?"

"Should I?"

"You're asking me?"

"Ella," I teased, "sometimes you really sound Jewish, you know that?"

"Sometimes I sound Jewish, sometimes I sound old, sometimes I don't even sound. So listen, if you see the man with the million dollars out there walking around looking lost, you'll show him where I live?"

"I might even take a cut of it myself."

"Take a cut." She smiled, but her eyes grew moist. "And if you see a woman looking older than she should walking around, too, you'll know it's my daughter. Tell her where I live, maybe she forgot. Tell her I've got a little cake I can always warm up."

Ella Crown stepped backward. She glanced at my coat, unable in that instant to look into my eyes.

"Maybe it would be better if I found Marilyn out there instead of the man with the million dollars," I said almost in a whisper.

"*Better* than the million dollars?" she exclaimed, staring at me with disbelief. "As *good* maybe, but not better. If the man with the million dollars is down there, you show them both up. Believe me, I'll find room for everybody."

Three

Unemployment: Peter and Marcus Rosenbloom

At the heart of all poverty areas is the enormous rate of unemployment. If the official national figures indicate that over 9 percent of the country's working force is out of work, then the rate in poor areas is double, triple, quadruple that. In some census tracts one finds unemployment running at as high as 75 percent. Of these unemployed people, many are what have been called "discouraged workers," men and women who have not worked in over two years and who have given up hope of finding work of any sort.

To be sure, there are some benefits accruing to the unemployed, usually in the form of insurance, which recently has diminished both in amount and in the period of time for which it runs. Thus, the unemployed turn to welfare, Social Security benefits, and, if possible, funds available to the elderly. But the destruction of the person and his or her family owing to unemployment is inestimable. It may well be the most crippling illness of poverty. It has been correlated with innumerable physical symptoms like stomach problems, headaches, tooth decay, as well as nervous disorders, impotence, and what is called antisocial behavior, namely theft, homicide, wife beating, child beating, even the battering of a woman when she is pregnant.

Like all who live in the poor communities of the United States, the Jews know the experience of unemployment. Like blacks and all the ethnic groups, they know the scenario of discrimination when it comes to finding jobs. They watch the young unable to find employment, they see no possibilities for the elderly to work, they see members of other communities landing the jobs to which they are perfectly suited. Granted, there are always cases of people refusing jobs that they feel are beneath them, if not openly degrading of their talents and competencies. But these cases are few. After a refusal or two, most all people accept whatever is offered to them. Again and again, one hears that expression: Beggars can't be choosers. Working in jobs that ill fit them is common among poor immigrant families, and particularly among those who survived the holocaust. While some survivors in fact found work in America comparable and even better than that which they pursued in their native countries, a large number of Jews were obliged to take what they could, even if it meant a total sacrifice of their former careers. Certainly it was common for the immigrants who flowed into the country in the 1940s to have to prove their worth all over again. For some, this was the quintessential hurt of being unemployed.

It goes without saying that to be out of work is to feel worthless. For good or bad, one's sense of self and the basis of one's judgment of self lie in one's work. When work is denied, the sense of personal worth declines, and in too many instances, the unemployed person is shunned by his or her very own family members. For like living in poverty, being unemployed strikes the affluent observer as being incredible to some degree. Yes, we say, poverty and unemployment are always with us, but how is it that I have done well but not my brother? How is it that this man survived under such wretched conditions, but his son cannot find work? Poverty is inevitable, surely, but not in *our* family.

Nowhere is the sense of personal failure higher than in the soul of the unemployed man or woman. The judgment of one's friends and family, one's society and culture, becomes internalized, until the circle is completed. I do not work, therefore I am a failure, and because I am a failure, there is no sense seeking work, for I would never get one of the few jobs available. All of this is experienced by poor unemployed Jews. They have one additional message as well, again from their friends, family, and culture: How is it, the message comes, that you, a Jew, are unable to find employment? Unthinkable! No matter how bleak the circumstances, how difficult the life, Jews have always been able to find work, or make work, and provide for themselves, without anybody's help. Jews ask for no favors, they help one another, they rely on no government. So how is it that *you* have not worked and for such a long time, too! Shameful. A disgrace!

Aaron and Sonia Rosenbloom first touched American soil in 1929, a few years before the Jews of their native Hungary began to feel the purges of the Nazi machine. Born in rural villages in Hungary, the Rosenblooms met in Budapest, where they were working. Both their sons, Marcus and Peter, were born in Budapest, and both resented deeply their parents' decision to immigrate to America. Marcus was nineteen at the time, Peter sixteen. Sonia Rosenbloom's cousins, the Feigelmans, had departed for the United States three years previously. In letters home they noted that America's streets were hardly paved with gold, but what could be worse than what we have known in Europe!

The Rosenblooms' immigration took them to Austria,

Venice, then on to Spain and finally a boat from Portugal, which arrived in New York in March of 1929. They lived in New York for several months, then moved to Philadelphia to join the Feigelmans. The move lasted two weeks. Unhappy in Philadelphia, they returned to New York, which has been the family's home ever since.

Peter Rosenbloom tells anybody who will listen to him that if he had a choice, he wouldn't be Jewish. "What has it gotten me all these years?" he asks. "Something special has come? Someone knocks on your door and says, 'Hello, stranger. Tell me, you're Jewish, 'cause if you are I've got a present for you that's going to make you so happy you're going to dance and sing, and play the banjo. You play the banjo, Rosenbloom? You don't, all right, so now you do. Look, here's a banjo, play me a song, called 'What I Have to Do to Find a Job.' Go on. Take the banjo in your hands, you'll find you can play it like an angel.' " Then Peter Rosenbloom looks away, embarrassed not only for his predicament but for making fun of himself, the predicament, life.

"The whole thing's not worth it. The whole thing stinks with a bad smell. I can't believe it's me sitting here, talking, making fun of the way I look, the way I sound, everything that's happening to me. Is this where I'm supposed to be? Is this what someone had in mind for me to be doing at my age? I'm sixty-two years old. You know what it means to be sixty-two years old? It means a lot more than in a few months I'll be sixty-three, I'll tell you. A lot more. What do you think they think of me, my family? You think they look at me and they're admiring what they see there, in this face, or what I do with myself? Or maybe they think, Ah, he's old, what can you expect? He's old, life's been hard on him. You think that's what they think? You want to know what *I* think? I think I don't care *what* they think because what *I* think is much worse than what they would ever think because it's me that's living this life. Right here, inside me. Believe me. I know exactly what's happening. A man is alive, he works; he's dead, he don't work. That's a formula. Not magic—a formula. A man is alive and he don't work, he's not in the formula, he's not a man. Believe me. I know. Fifteen years now I'm not working. Fifteen years, not a single thing I can say I earned with these hands. Fifteen years of my family looking at me and saying to themselves, This Rosenbloom, what is he, some kind of a fish, or a stone maybe? Maybe he's a stone who sits around all day not doing anything. A big, ugly stone. You push him here, you push him there, you get out of him what you get out of a stone. You get blood out of a stone? You don't work all these years, you're a stone. That's what they're thinking, and that's what I'm thinking."

Peter Rosenbloom's father always insisted the family was lucky to have been able to come to America. Not everybody got that chance. Aaron Rosenbloom warned his two sons that while the stories of American riches were exaggerated, there was some truth to them. Many immigrants had arrived penniless and within a few years were living in big houses, driving big cars, and having people look up to them, in a double sense. For not only had they proven themselves to be successful in a country that worships success, he said, but they were successful after having started with nothing at all. America was just like everyone described it, Aaron Rosenbloom had told his sons, a land of opportunity. That didn't mean getting anything free. But it did mean the jobs were there, the work possibilities plentiful. What a person did with these possibilities was *their* business. You worked hard in America, you'd see, it would pay off. The serious problem, Peter Rosenbloom's father said again and again, was whether immigrants like themselves were big enough and strong enough to deal with their being successful, or not being successful, because that could happen, too. There was no bigger move a person could make than leave the country where he was born; leave the people he had known all his life, learn a new language and prove to different people that he was a real man who could work not only as good as the next guy but *better* than him. Because, he told his sons, they'll always be looking at you differently from how they look at their own. It will always be different.

Aaron Rosenbloom found work in America. The wages were hardly as fat as he imagined them to be, but he did find work, and he went to his grave telling his sons that no one could see him as anything but a success. His wife agreed. While he never earned more than nine thousand dollars a year, the fact was that the family lived in only one city, and in only two apartments, the first for less than six months. Anybody judging the Rosenblooms had to say they were stable, steady people, and how else could success be defined? Aaron Rosenbloom died when Peter was in his late thirties, his brother Marcus a few years older.

Sonia Rosenbloom, a sickly woman, never recovered from the sadness and emptiness she felt on the passing of her husband. Nor did her uncertainty about the move to America, an uncertainty she never revealed to her husband, help her to feel strong and resolute about her future. Money wasn't a problem. Her husband had left some insurance money; she would make out. Her sons gave her some pleasure, although she worried about both of them, especially Peter. His education had never been what it should have, and he never seemed to take to America. He was like her in that regard. Marcus was like his father. If Marcus had regrets about leaving his native land when he was nineteen, he never showed it. He assumed the same spirit of challenge his father espoused and made a successful life for himself in a copper pipe company. That his wife's father had a few connections didn't hurt any. Marcus Rosenbloom was the success his father needed to prove that the decision to leave Hungary had been a wise one.

Every Sunday the elder Rosenblooms lunched with Marcus and his wife, Sarah. That was a ritual. Peter was always invited but he rarely came. What did it matter? It didn't take Peter's presence to confirm Marcus' great success. "It takes a generation," Sonia Rosenbloom heard her husband say every Sunday night. "*That's* a success. A generation. And Peter will come around. Maybe not while I'm here to see it, but he'll come around."

Peter Rosenbloom always felt closer to his mother than his father. He would adjust to America, he insisted when she asked him if he was happy, which was often because she saw in him signs of discontent. He was not faring well in the new country. Driving a taxicab part-time, starting and stopping with school, not getting married, they were indications that Peter was having problems. He seemed to have no close friends, he rarely went out. An exception was his regular appearance at Friday night dinner, not that the Rosenblooms were so religious. It was nice that he came, and it was nice that he said he came because it meant a lot to his father, but his mother knew that he had nothing better to do and maybe, too, he was anxious about moving away from his parents. So she worried about him, and the little he told her about his life didn't make her worry any less. There was no hiding the fact that they were best friends who shared many things, the most important being the realization that neither of them could ever consider themselves Americans. "Your brother's Mr. America," Peter's mother would tell him, "but you belong in Europe. Maybe you should go back. What was right, maybe, for your father and your brother doesn't have to be right for you."

"How many times we discussed my leaving America, me and that sweet lady," Peter Rosenbloom remembers, thinking back over more than thirty years. "How many times. She knew, I knew. It was the work. She saw it all in my work. You come all the way from Budapest to drive a taxi? That's what my father had in his mind when he left? To see a son drive a taxi? And how long was that going to last? Everybody thinks, you got nothing else to do, *nu*, you'll drive a taxi. How bad can it be? You buy a map and every day you get the paper before anybody else does so you can make conversation with the fares, you know what I mean. How terrible is that? You think people ever wonder about a taxi driver? What his life is like? They figure they give him a big tip, that's a hard way to live? Look at the meter, look at the meter, five dollars for a few minutes' work, how bad can it be? They worry, all these people, how little you keep? I don't want to talk about it. It's over. It's fifteen years since I did it. So I'm on welfare, with a lot of other people, and my parents are dead so they don't know, and my brother Marcus thinks I'm a bum, and if his children aren't sure what they're supposed to think about me, he makes sure every night to tell them how their Uncle Peter is an unemployed bum, a big stone.

"You want to know about my brother Marcus, Tom, I'll tell you a story. Ten years ago he comes to me. Calls me up one night and tells me we have to talk. 'Such a mystery,' I told him. 'What are we going to do, invest a million dollars somewhere?' You should have heard him. 'We have to talk, we have to talk.' 'Okay, so come over and we'll talk.' 'I'm not coming by your home,' he says. '*Nu*,' I tell him, 'I'll come to you.' 'No, you're not coming to me either.' I wasn't good enough, see. Wait, you'll hear the story. So we meet, just like he says, in this place, a little restaurant. I know where it is. It's a perfect meeting place because it's a million miles from where both of us live. He's got it all figured out perfect. No one in his neighborhood should see me with him, and he wouldn't be caught dead in my neighborhood. So we meet in this restaurant. All right, so I don't argue. Why should I argue? How do I know what he wants? Maybe he wants a loan. Maybe he wants to cut into my welfare check.

"So the next thing I know we're sitting in this restaurant where he's never been and I've never been. What's he after? Are you ready? 'Peter,' he tells me, like he was the President of the

United States, 'we've got a little problem.' *He's* telling me *we've* got a problem? Him in his big house, me without a job, and he's telling *me we've* got a problem. *Nu*, what's the problem? 'You know my wife Sarah,' he says. 'No, I don't know your wife Sarah. Of course I know your wife Sarah. What kind of a question is that?' I'm thinking, know her, yes; like her, no. She's a *shnorer*. You know who Sarah Rosenbloom is? She's a person who ten minutes after you give her a ten-thousand-dollar diamond ring, she's fishing in your pants, maybe she can find a five-dollar bill. And she'll settle for a little loose change. 'Yeah, I'm acquainted with this woman you mention.' 'Don't be so fresh,' he tells me. 'I'm not fresh, but what kind of a question?' 'All right,' he says, 'so you don't know all her relations.' 'No, I don't know her side of the family,' which is the only side because it's ten years my parents are dead and I'm as good as dead in their eyes because I don't work, so who's on our side? Nobody. All her people are both sides of the family. If they got married today, I'd be the only one on my side of the *shul*. I should say, my side of the aisle because Marcus Rosenbloom doesn't know from *shuls*, he knows only from getting married in swanky hotels.

"So what does he want from me, my wise considerate brother, here in this tenth-class restaurant? You can guess. You can also guess that when we're done, which we're going to be in a very short time, that he's going to insist on paying the bill, all dollar-fifty of it. Marcus Rosenbloom the rich Hungarian turned one hundred percent American. Mr. Yank. 'So, Marcus, tell me, you're ashamed I don't work.' Oh, he knows I try all the time to find work, but facts are facts, I don't work, I collect welfare. It's a big shame. '*Nu*, what do I do?' I ask him. Well, he says, he knows it's not my fault. Still, it doesn't look so good to some people that he's got a brother who in his heyday was a taxi driver. In his heyday. And now, in his not so heyday, is doing nothing. Sitting all day long. 'You want to give me money?' I ask him. No. No money. 'You want I should tell people I'm president of a bank?' Already I guessed what he wanted. Either I'm supposed to change my name or move away. Probably number two. He's going to give me money for transportation, an airplane ride, anywhere I want, but it just doesn't look good on Sarah's side of the family for him to have a slob for a brother. Being out of work, *they've* decided, doesn't look good. It reflects on the family and affects the children. How *I* feel about it, how *I'm* suffering inside and have nobody to talk to because after my mother died there was nobody, this they aren't interested in. Twenty million times my brother talked to me, always with one question. Not, how are you feeling? Did you find something yet? When my mother was alive, he had another question, How's Mamma? because after my father died he didn't have time for her because his wife, the great human being, while she wasn't fishing in his pockets for spending money, she was whispering in his ear that maybe they'd had enough with her mother-in-law. And anyway, Peter the bum could look out for his mother since they had in common the fact they were both out of work. I'm sure it went that way. I know it. He wouldn't have turned his back on his own mother otherwise.

"So now he's pushing me out of town. I can go anywhere I like, but I'm going. Like I won a prize on a television show, *they're* sending me out of the city. He's going to write to me, call me, help me get settled. It couldn't be better from his point of view. The shame is less with me away. The farther away I go, the easier it will be for all of them. Marvelous, isn't it? I wasn't even surprised. That's the kind of person he was. I say it just that way because as big a *shnorer* as *she* was, *he* has to be weak to let her put him up to that. So I told him, 'Go away? I wouldn't go away if you put me in a palace. *I* want to go away, *I'll* go away. *You* want me to go away, what are you, the government extraditing me? What am I, a crook that's making trouble for people? I'm a sick man with nothing in my life but a two-room apartment and an $83.65 welfare check and I can't find work. I'll drive a taxi anytime they want, any hour, any day, Saturday, Sunday, Christmas, Pesach, anytime, but they don't want me. So what am I supposed to do, sue them? Take them to court? But go away? Never. Not by your command, not by your wife's command, not from nobody. I don't break the law.' But Marcus is waiting for me. Like a cat. He knows what I'm going to answer even before I'm answering. Maybe in the little goodness it would be nice to think he has, he wants me to say no. But I don't care *what* he thinks because he's not moving *me* out or anybody else. If he's so ashamed of me for being unemployed—or maybe he doesn't like the idea that I'm robbing the country with my welfare check or that I'll be richer than him someday on eighty-some bucks—but if it bothers him so much and his wife, then let *them* move. Let *them* tell their children, 'We're so ashamed of that bum, that stone who we refuse to let you see, we're moving. And you should always remember one thing: That man you used to call your uncle, he's not really your uncle. By pure chance, by pure chance, he happens to have the same last name like you. Maybe by pure chance he happens to have the same parents as your father, but that doesn't mean a thing.'

"All right. So I give him my answer. And he's back at me in a flash. 'So maybe you could change your name,' he says. 'In fact, even better, you could take back the name we once had in Hungary.' So again I have my answer waiting for him. 'You don't like the name, *you* change it.' Can you imagine all this happening just because I'm not working? The word of the century is 'unemployed.' Nobody's surprised to find out that anybody's unemployed. It's everywhere. Rich, middle, poor. You always got people who don't want to work but I'm talking now about when you can't *find* work. It's everywhere. It's like people with false teeth. Millions of people have them. Sometimes you can tell right off, sometimes you don't know. They hide it. It's the same with unemployment. What, are you going to be ashamed about it? How can you be ashamed? You prayed that your teeth would fall out? You asked somebody to knock them out of your head? It just happened. So you do the best. You don't announce, How do you? Here, you like my dentures, I'll take them out, you can study them. But you also don't throw people away or hide them because they got a serious problem. What do they think, these pocket pickers like my sister-in-law? That we like to go without work? What have they got in this country, ten million people out of work? More? And we're supposed to like it? You don't like false teeth. You don't like being in public and wondering whether they're going to fall out in your soup, and you don't like being all by yourself, and see them sitting there in a glass. You know you're not working. People don't have to come around and have secret meetings in tenth-class restaurants to tell you. 'How do you explain it?' my brother asks me. How do you explain it? Like I'm a little baby.

"So how *do* I explain it? 'I don't work. If it's shameful to you, then it's shameful to me ten thousand and ten!' If it's hurting his reputation with his family, what's it doing to my heart? 'Can you explain *that* to me?' I asked him. 'I'm sure it hurts, I'm sure it hurts.' That's his answer. Yeah, it hurts me so much he wants me to change my name. So I'll become Jake Epstein and it won't hurt anymore? Or maybe I could become Franklin Roosevelt and they'll make me President. What is it with people like this? They believe only in money and magic. Change your name, fill the pockets with money and magic, you're a rich man. It doesn't work like that. Believe me. If magic could have got me a job, any job, not just driving a taxi, I'd have found that magic a long time ago.

"There we sat, drinking coffee, my brother and me. Each with our own pewter pot. Ten years ago but I remember it like yesterday. I told myself, don't tell him nothing more than you have to. He's like a boxer. He's looking for my weaknesses. My own brother, huh? 'So you won't move, eh?' 'No, I'm not moving. I'm not changing. You got a job for me, we'll talk. You don't want me to see your family because you're ashamed, that problem's already settled: You'll never see me. What do they say? I'll never darken your door! 'I should give you a job?' he says to me. Suddenly, *he's* angry like *I* was the one who wanted to send *him* away. I should have told him, Marcus, I'm ashamed of you for working when I don't have a job. You're a shame to an unemployed man like me. And there he is behind his little pewter coffeepot shouting at me: '*I* should give *you* a job? *Chutzpah* like this I've never heard in my life.' So while he's looking like a boxer for my weakness, he's made his mistake and I have *his* weakness.

" 'Marcus,' I tell him, 'that you even say the word *chutzpah* is the biggest *chutzpah* you could ever know. You think there are clubs for unemployed people? And if there were, you think I'd join? I wouldn't be caught dead talking to people like me. What are they going to tell me I don't already know better than all of them? 'Marcus, I got a question for you: how come you stopped speaking Yiddish? How come that is? How come when the few times you talked to your mother she spoke Yiddish and you answered in English? Not even Hungarian. Huh? How come it was that she cried to me about you all those nights you didn't have time for her 'cause your debt was paid off to your father? What about *that*, Mr. Yankee America? How come *you're* ashamed of me and *I'm* ashamed of you *and* your work, a hundred hours a week of it for all I know?' What I wanted to tell him I couldn't tell him. With a wife like his I'd work two hundred hours a week. Even if she took all my money it'd be better working than sitting home with her or lying in the bed watching her fish through my pants pockets. *Nu*, Sarah, don't forget to look in his vests. Men like my brother always have a little something tucked away in the vest.

" 'So, Marcus,' I'm telling him in the secret restaurant, 'don't *you* tell me about unemployment because I'll tell you something about life that's far more important. I'll tell you about history, about forgetting where you came from, what your parents and grandparents were, and did, for you, my such a grown-up brother. That's for number one. And I'll tell you about being loyal to your family. Not just your wife and that group of lovelies she calls her family who couldn't be so great if they work so hard to yank you away from your own family. That's for number two. And for number three, what about a little dignity maybe, for the first, second, and third temple? What do you think, Marcus, you could have a little respect for the people here and there who maybe died or hid or felt terrible about being alive so that people like you could ask for secret meetings with people like me and plan ways to get rid of them?'

"Was I giving it to him, him, Marcus, the boy who beat me up so many times in my life I'm probably still black and blue if I ever had the courage to take a look where he hit me. But you know, Tom, he was listening. He was listening but good. I'm his brother. He knew who was talking to him, and he knew I was one hundred percent right about everything I told him. The history, the coming from Hungary here, our father, our mother being sick and he came, what, three, four times a year to look in on her. That's what I told him. 'You looked in, like a doctor looks in because if he spends too much time, if he talks a little with someone, and makes them feel like a human being, he'll lose money. She knew you were too busy for her.' You know what she told me? She told me for only one reason did she want me to get work. One reason. Make enough money to go back to Europe. Nothing about me being happy or feeling good, just take her home. She was never at home here. My father wanted to come here, she came, she didn't want to. You know what she told me, and all this I'm telling Mr. Successful who's listening, too, and I mean but good. In fact, I began to think, I'm living alone and have nobody to talk to, and this man's living in a family it seems like there's ten thousand of them and *he's* got nobody to talk to. I told him, 'Your mother held on to one thing when she came here, Yiddish. She spoke Yiddish with your father and with me. On her deathbed, you remember on her deathbed when you finally found ten minutes

75

to make a visit? Yiddish. Always Yiddish. And you use the word *chutzpah* like you spoke it every day.' I told him, 'It's true, Marcus, I haven't worked. I haven't worked in five years and the chances of me ever finding work are lousy. And you'll work 'til you drop which I hope won't be for a long, long time. But I got dignity, and you haven't. All you got is a job, but I know my place, my position, and I don't care what *anybody* says about unemployed people. I know the important things, all you know is the buck, and nine to five, and doing what everybody wants you to do no matter what *you* think about it. You shouldn't have quit on your mother so soon!"

"He comes back at me, my brother, because he's not dumb. 'What,' he's yelling at me, 'you *like* not working? You're proud that you don't work? You don't think I'm good at my job and a good family man?'

" 'I *hate* that I don't work. What do you want me to tell you?' I told him. 'I cry every night. Every night. Okay? You happy now? I'd beg on the streets in *your* neighborhood, *my* neighborhood, in the middle of downtown if I thought it would do any good. I'd walk around in front of a bunch of children with my teeth in a glass if it made them laugh and I got paid for it. What are you telling me I'm proud? I'm proud of nothing in my life. Nothing at all. I wasn't so proud when I did drive the taxi. What was so great about *that*? I'd like to know. Everybody asking me questions like I was a professor. What do you think about the President doing this or doing that, or Senator this one or that one? What's to be proud? I'm ashamed. Of course, I'm ashamed. You think I need a secret meeting with you like we were two spies or something to remind me that I'm sick from not being able to find work? You think it's good how I live, where I live, that I even live? Who knows me better than you? Who knows how I feel better than you, and you come here ready to shove me like baggage into the first plane? You want to send me away, Marcus, all right, I've changed my mind, send me. Look at me. Everything worth owning is what you see. Put me on a plane, right now, I don't need to pack anything. Not a toothbrush, nothing. You want to laugh, Marcus, here's a laugh for you, for free. I don't even own a suitcase. You got Mamma's. So send me. Go ahead, send me. I'm ready. America is getting rid of its unemployed men, you're just doing your share. That's what people will say, so you don't have to worry. The problem of unemployment starts at home, you're just doing your little bit to clean up the problem. Huh? Someone asks, what did you do for unemployment in your company, Mr. Rosenbloom? *Nu*, you'll tell him, in the company nothing, but I shipped my brother to the West Coast. Now *they* got the problem.'

"So there's my poor, rich brother, the man I know in my heart isn't happy in Hungary or here or anywhere, 'cause he's just like me and is afraid to admit it even to himself, and he's crying and he's laughing. And I'm beginning to laugh and cry a little myself. 'Peter,' he says, 'tell me, you have a good dentist?' I told him, 'Who needs a dentist, I need teeth.' 'Is there any chance,' he asks me, 'that you could find work maybe in another part of the city?' Maybe I should move myself, not out of the city, but out to someplace new. 'I look every day,' I told him. Every day. My job in life is to find a job.' 'You got friends?' he asks. 'You want the truth, Marcus? Only you.' 'You got me,' he says. I remember, he pushes the little pewter pot away and touches my hand. We're both crying. It's all like a movie. And I felt a little proud, not so much that I could forget even in that wonderful moment when I saw how much he loved me and I saw too how in all the world he's the only one I have, even with that pocket fisher of a wife he's got, but not so proud that I could forget that when I would leave him I'd still be a man without a job. Not that proud. *That* you don't forget. In the day, the night, it's always there.

"I'll tell you something I don't feel so proud about, something I never did tell my brother. I didn't go to temple for four years when I lost my job. *That* much ashamed I was. Isn't that something for the books? I couldn't go. I couldn't sit there and go through the motions and make believe that everything in my life was going so well. I *still* don't go to temple with a free conscience. I'm like a criminal, like I did something and I can't go into a place of worship pretending. I can't be there with the feeling I'm hiding something. It doesn't make sense, but that's how it is. That's something I couldn't tell my brother, which shows how sad it was between us, and what not working has done to me, *and* to him, *and* to his wife who spends all day on the telephone telling her family what a monster her husband has for a brother. First she kept him away from my mother, now it's me she can't stand.

"Well, what can you do?" Peter Rosenbloom was standing up in the living room of his small apartment, looking at the objects he had collected. He didn't seem particularly sad, or happy, particularly anything for that matter. He was merely looking. "Maybe that secret lunch with my brother was the highlight of the last ten years. That and a couple of funerals and that about takes care of my social life. Put it all together with a little shame and the feeling that what's the sense of going on, and that's my whole life. I'll tell you, nobody likes to see himself as a failure. You think people like standing in front of a mirror and pointing a finger and saying, 'Morris, you're a bum! You're Morris the Bum!' Nobody likes to say that. Jewish, Gentile, who wants to see that in the mirror? Not from yourself, not from your brother, from nobody do you want to hear what you are, unless they got good things to say. Move away, change my name, disappear, all right, so now I'm invisible, so they got jobs for invisible people like me? They want me to be invisible, that's what they want. That I should go away and leave them with their memories. Oh, that Peter Rosenbloom, what a wonderful man he was, what a wonderful person. Didn't work for fifteen years but did it matter to anyone? Not in the slightest. Because even with the false teeth and the nothing apartment and the few hours he drove a taxi, which is below him, naturally, he was wonderful to his brother and his mother and father and his little nephew and niece. I mean, this was a good man. You hear them saying all this? I hear them every day of my life. So he didn't work, so whose fault was it that America fell apart and all the Peter Rosenblooms couldn't get a job for love nor money? Was it *his* fault? Not on your life. He was a beautiful man. Gorgeous, handsome, no job, but beautiful.

"You want to know where all this leaves me? I'm a double bum. Bum number one because I'm not working like a good Jewish man, and bum number two because I'm not working in the right profession or the right business. You think my sister-in-law thinks like that? You can be sure she thinks like that. Fellow walks up to her and says, 'How do you do, my job is to kill Jews like your husband and his brother.' 'Tell me,' she says, 'that's steady work that pays well? You go to college to learn that?' 'Of course it's steady work. Of course you go to college, 'til you're thirty years old. What, you think they'll teach anybody how to kill Jews?' '*Nu,*' she'd say, 'if you're working regular and you've finished with college, how bad a person can you be? No matter how bad, you can't be as bad as my brother-in-law, because he doesn't work at all. And he's going to die before he finds a job.'

"She's not a Jew. And my brother isn't either. Should I tell you what they are? They're nothing. They're not us, they're not them, because they don't feel. She never did, and once he did, but she took care of that for him but good. You know what they should be doing? They should be helping me, supporting me, making out like I'm wanted in their home. People do that for you in this neighborhood even if they don't have a job or ten cents they can spare. They aren't even Jewish, ninety percent of them. You think there's a lot of us here? There's very few, but all of us hold together, even if we don't say anything to anybody half the time. We hold together. We have our jobs to do, only the Rosenblooms on the other side of this city can't see what we do. They should look a little closer one of these days, and they'd see we got first the job of trying to find a job. Then we got two, the job of surviving. They don't see that, because it's too big for them, and we're too small for them. You want the truth? We're better without them, without their suggestions about what we should do. We'll be fine without them. As far as they're concerned we're all without faces and names, and we got no feelings, no pride, nothing we remember. They want to feel like that, I say that's fine with me. They want to judge a person on whether he's got a job, let them go right ahead. I wouldn't stop them if I had the power. Fact is, I'm too busy these days even to think of them.

"You know what all this time without work does to a person? What's the word I want? It warps us? Is that it? Makes us different from what we are. I don't think about my brother every day of my life? I don't think about his wife and his children every day of my life? As much as I think she's the world's biggest nothing, the biggest thief, phony baloney in the country, I don't want to be invited by her, by *her* not him, to dinner, once in a while, once a week maybe? I don't think what it would feel like to drive a car I own up to their home and carry in some flowers and a little bottle of wine and some nice little somethings for the kids? I don't think that? Or that they'd ask me about my job and I'd tell them well, you know business, Marcus, and you know, too, Sarah darling, because you talk to your husband, some days you make a dollar, some days you lose a dollar, but in the end we all make out all right? And they could see just by looking that I make out a whole lot more than just all right. I don't want the chance to take a drink of the wine I brought, give thanks that we're all healthy and the kids are growing nice and let out a big sigh and say, *Nu*, things could be worse? I could be unemployed. And everybody would laugh. Even the children. I don't want that? Of course I want that. That's *all* I want, all I've ever wanted even with all the closeness of my mother. A man comes to the door right now and says,

'Rosenbloom, you can have that, just like you told it. The price? Give me your eyes.' I tell him, 'I can sit at my brother's table, Sarah's table, with a suit, with the presents, the wine, the whole deal, you'll give me that and a regular job, and I give you my eyesight?' You know what I tell him? 'Take my eyes, my ears, my hands, my feet. Take everything you want. Everything, from top to bottom. It's yours.' *That's* how much I think about them, there on the other side of the city.

"It could be funny, you know. It could be a wonderful comedy. It could be that like magic this man, let's call him Elijah, walks in here and gives a look like, What, Rosenbloom, all these years and all you got is two rooms, and makes his proposition about I'll take your eyes and I'll give you the job and suits and the wine and flowers. It could be very funny because it could end up that after giving me all he promised, when he wants to collect from me, he finds he can't get a thing 'cause after all these years of not working I have nothing left to give, not even my eyes. Couldn't somebody somewhere find that very funny? A person with a job I mean."

Four

Changing Neighborhoods: Johnnie Murphy and Mr. Klein

Every sociological study made on communities where the poor live reveals shifts in population and corresponding changes in the character of these communities. Over a time, one inevitably sees groups of people coming into a particular neighborhood, other groups moving out, although not before some degree of assimilation, however slight, has taken place. The move out may be total, in that the location of home and business is transferred. In other cases, residence is changed, but the business stays behind.

Residents of most every city are able to pinpoint local Italian, Portuguese, Greek, Armenian, Chinese, black, Jewish communities, all of which seem to border on one another. Typically, these special communities are the ones that give "character" and "personality" to the city. Most urban dwellers, moreover, know a bit of the history of the various neighborhoods, how the Jews live here, but they used to live there. They moved out when this group or that group moved in. Those of us living in cities know, too, how particular urban renewal programs forced certain groups out of their old neighborhoods and into neighborhoods more or less congenial to them. In fact, as we take stock of some of these programs, we are not always certain what exactly *did* happen to a particular population of people. They seemed to have disappeared. We say, for example, the Jews moved from this area to that area, but what we mean is that the more affluent moved, for the poorer ones either stayed or moved to other areas which in fact were not much better than the neighborhoods they knew previously.

Strangely, as these hundreds of American communities change, and as the social scientists and journalists record and account for these changes, one finds a great number of people living not only where they lived as children but where their parents lived as well. One's residence may have changed, but one has not left "the old neighborhood." Indeed, poor families travel outside their own neighborhood very little. Fifty streets away may seem to them as gigantic a move as the more affluent American considers travel to Europe.

All of this is well known, scientifically documented, part of Americans' common knowledge about themselves and the so-called melting pot culture they share. The irony is that those who travel little, who see their neighborhood changing in real and dramatic ways, are themselves attached to the very European and Asian and African cultures that so many affluent families have listed for summer travel. Furthermore, the Jews, like some of their counterparts in the poorer communities, are particularly sensitive to shifts in population and the corresponding rearrangements in political and economic relationships. The arrival of a new group threatens a sense of group purity to some, the very existence of that group to others. For immigrants, and especially survivors of the holocaust, the image of people packing and moving on is one of the most terrifying of all human impressions. Merely living is a sufficiently temporary affair; for some people, the temporariness is comprised only of precarious moments.

The stories of what happens to people in the course of their neighborhood changing are known to everyone living in these neighborhoods. The story of a neighbor's fate is often as disturbing as the story of one's own personal evolution. What follows is one of these stories.

Johnnie Murphy's parents came from Ireland when they were in their early teens. The time was 1910. Johnnie's father was from County Sligo, his mother from County Mayo. Both families had settled in South Boston, where Johnnie and his six brothers, second-generation Americans, were to be born and raised. It was not far from his birthplace that Johnnie Murphy established his friendship with a man he simply called Klein.

Very little is known of Klein's life. It was said by neighbors that both he and his wife were immigrants from Germany, or was it Austria? It was also said that he spoke four or five languages, so presumably he had traveled a great deal in Europe. Two things were certain: His native language was Yiddish, and he came to America either during World War II or immediately afterward. A child was born to the Kleins in the United States. Or perhaps it was two children. . . .

Johnnie Murphy is fifty-five years old. A short man, strongly built, with pink cheeks, a nose that has been flattened, he says, from fights, and soft white hair, he has lived within the same ten-block area for almost his entire life. During World War II he fought in France and Germany. Several years ago, he took his wife and three children to Canada on a fishing trip. He saved his money a long time for that trip, and he hopes to make another one to the same towns. His jobs over the last twenty years have changed, he says, almost with the season. "You name it, I've done it. Or been fired from it."

Johnnie Murphy calls himself a happy man. His nature is

to be content with what he has, make the best of what is available. His greatest fear is unemployment; his greatest sadness, what he calls the decline of his country, the decaying of America's cities. It's all found in the changing character of neighborhoods. "Oh," he will say, his gentle blue eyes moving quickly, "the changes don't *have* to be for the worse, but they always turn out that way, because people haven't learned how to be kind. All they know is how to be rough. What the hell, I know it myself. Love to have a dollar for every time this old nose got socked in a fight. All of them worth fighting at the time, none of them worth a goddamn thing ten minutes after they was over. We're rough, like animals. Old, young, a bunch of raging animals. But some of us is worse than others, if you get my meaning. Stay around here for a couple of weeks and you'll see for yourself. Sound like a TV show I'm talking about? Ain't no TV show, buddy boy, though I wonder how much some of these people begin to take things from what they see on the TV. TV's teaching too many people too many things they'd be better off not knowing. Thing that gets me is how innocent people get hurt when the neighborhoods change. That's the thing you want to worry yourself about most. You go looking for a fight, you're going to find one, you see what I mean. But what about all these people who run from fights and get hurt all the same?"

Johnnie Murphy sits at a corner table in a Pickney Street bar. He stares at the foam of his beer holding to the side of the tall glass. Then he rubs one eye hard. There is anger in his manner; he cannot stop the itching. He turns his head sharply, looking down the line of the wall, then stares back into the glass. And he tells this story:

"This guy I knew, Klein, was a funny little fat pudgy sort of a guy. Each year, it struck me, he got a little bit shorter. Or maybe he began to lean over. Knew him, let's see, must be at least fifteen years. I saw him two, three times a week. Kind of a guy you see in the beginning, you don't say much to, but after a couple years you become friends, but not real friends. It's hard to explain. Call him an associate. Guy and his wife owned a little food store, terrible location, near nobody, and four blocks away they're putting in a giant of a supermarket. You see where I'm getting? For years, this guy and his wife been holding on by the skin of their teeth. People like me, we do all our shopping in his store. Why not? It's clean, he's got good produce, so what if he don't have everything we need? I like the guy. First, it's just hello, how are you? Then, pretty soon, it's talk about my family and his family. He knows my name, I know his name, though I can't pronounce his first name too good, but he doesn't say nothing about it. He could correct me 'cause I can hear he says it different from me. Couple of years of how are you, and I'm going in regular to talk. He tells me about his business, how the prices are killing him, making him stop getting certain items which is always the items people want. Then he's got all these problems with his inventory, what he's got, what he don't have. How can you tell, the stuff comes in, the stuff goes out.

"So now let's see. 'Bout seven years ago, I'm laid off from a job I had delivering firewood in the suburbs, and I'm in with Klein, just hanging around, and he comes up to me, a sweet guy, I mean it. He says, 'Murphy.' I'm Murphy to him, he's Klein to me, like he should never forget I'm Irish and I'm never going to forget he's Jewish. 'Murphy,' he says, 'what's wrong?' So what's wrong, that's the way he talked. Like sometime he'd like sing it. 'Nothing's wrong,' I told him, 'though I was really down. April, you know, no job, no good prospects lined up. You don't like facing the old lady. So Klein says, 'Don't tell me there's nothing wrong, I'm reading it on your face.' I told him about my job and he says, 'Come with me.' So we go in the back of the store, and I'm surprised it's so small. I never been in the back before but I was expecting it to be large, like he had a warehouse or something. But it's nothing. Boxes stacked up everywhere. There was no place to sit down. I saw his wife wasn't there so I said, 'Where's your wife?' 'She's sick,' he says.

'Don't worry.' 'So how can we come back here when you may have customers and other people coming in?' You notice I say customers and other people. Other people means two things. First off, because he's in the neighborhood so long, and because he's the kind of guy he is, he's got other people like me dropping in to talk with him, even though we're always in his way. Just standing there we're in his way, 'cause with the store so small, and the way he's got it laid out, there's barely room for anybody in there. But he's got people coming in all the time to talk, sit around, and be comfortable. And everybody who comes, he'd say, in that way he spoke, 'Here, take an apple. Take a pear. Take something, for Chrissake. You afraid I'll charge you? Don't worry, I won't charge you. Here, I'll eat an apple with you if it's going to make you feel better about it.' That's the way he talked; that's the way he was. You had to know him. This was a sweet man.

"Now, the other type of, what do you want to call them, noncustomers he had, were kids coming in there to steal. Not only kids, everybody. I saw a cop once snatch a box of raisins. You believe that? What's that going to cost? Twenty cents tops, right? Klein saw him. We watched the cop together. When he left I looked at him the same time he looked at me. 'You going to let him get away with that?' I mean I was ready to go after the son of a bitch myself. So Klein says, 'What do you want me to do, call *another* cop? Isn't it bad enough this one's got my raisins? I'll call another cop he'll take a melon.' It was true, what could he do? Some of the kids who came in there, you never saw such a bunch of animals in your life. You'd see a little innocent-looking boy come in there, you know, 'Good morning, Mr. Klein,' he'd say, and Klein, he'd know the kid's name. Then the kid pulls out his shopping list, you know. 'My mother wants a half pound of sugar, three lemons,' and on and on, and while Klein's getting what the kid wants, the kid's stuffing his pockets with candy, grapes, cookies, anything he can find. I caught this kid stealing in there one night, you know. I beat him to an inch of his life. I made him give the stuff back. Klein, he knows what's going on, but he's concerned about the kid's bleeding on the cheek, where I popped him myself. *He's* bandaging the kid up while I'm emptying his pockets of the stuff he took two minutes before from the guy who's taking care of him. Can you imagine this scene? Somebody told me that, I'd say you're crazy; you're making the whole thing up. And you know damn well a week later the same kid will be right back in that shop with Klein doing the same thing, with his little list, stealing the Jew blind if guys like me weren't there. I told Klein, 'Give me a few bucks and I'll guard the store for you.' He told me, 'I'll give you a few bucks and you can come here and visit me. Don't guard nothing!'

"Then, of course, he had the real toughies. Miserable punks. They didn't have no little lists. They'd just pop in the door, snatch something, and wham, they're gone. Maybe not much each time, but something. Every day something. Enough of them do that it cuts into your stock. Takes one helluva lot of money out of your pocket. Klein figured it up one day. I told him. 'Don't it bother you, all these kids barging in here like that, taking whatever they want?' These kids wasn't content just to pocket a couple of apples, either. They had to make sure they called him a name before they left. Some of them, they'd call him the Nazi. Can you imagine? They call *him* Nazi? Hey, listen, I was in Germany in '43 and '44, I saw what the Nazi and the Jewish thing was all about. They call *him* Nazi? That has to be the irony of the century. 'Get a cop in here,' I told him. 'Get a guard. I'll do it for you myself. I don't give a damn if it's my own son doing it, I'll break his face open. Don't stand for that, Klein.' I don't know how many times I told him, 'Don't stand for it!'

" 'What do you want me to do?' That's the way he always said it, too. He'd bring his shoulders up. 'I'm sixty-seven. I'll call a cop, he'll steal my raisins. You think the governor's going to use his important policemen as a bodyguard for Klein's grocery?' He was right, too. He wrote letters to the precinct station about the kids. And let me tell you there was black kids and white kids. I'd love to tell you it was only black kids, but it was both. And girls. Just as much as boys. Always the tough one: 'Come on, come on, don't be afraid, take all the stuff he's got. He's just an old man.' Then the one who's always afraid: 'You think we should? It ain't right. Maybe we'll get caught.' But those kind always find ways of making the weak ones go along. I was one of those tough ones once. God Almighty, I stole my share when I was a kid. Not from no Jew either, but from a good old Irish family name of Tierney. Stole 'em blind. Old man Tierney, he caught me this one time and beat the living Jesus out of me. I didn't go near his shop again. That's why I told Klein, he's got to get tough with 'em. But he's not going to do it. All you have to do is look at the guy and you know he ain't the type to get rough. He was old, and always sort of sickly, with his little cough. His wife wasn't bigger than a flea herself. I told him, 'I'll do it, I'll do it.' 'What's to do?' he'd say. 'So they'll steal. And when they steal everything I have, I'll pack up and go away, and they'll steal from the next one. I'm too old to fight this kind of war.'

"I felt so bad for the guy when he talked like that, because he was right. The neighborhood was going to hell. Maybe the whole city was, for that matter. The Irish and the Italians and the Jews, they had their wars. It wasn't beautiful sweet music all the time in the old neighborhoods. Don't let nobody fool you into believing that. But we made it through. We made it until the Negroes came in. Then the wars *really* started. Then we needed each other. Sure, I'd look out for my own kind, but I'd look out to protect any decent person who wasn't causing trouble, black or white, Jew or no Jew. And this guy Klein was causing no one trouble. This man didn't know the meaning of the word 'enemy.' All he did was give, give, give, and instead of people liking him for it, they took advantage of him. They stepped all over him.

"That's why I told him when I went in the back of the store with him that first time, 'Listen, Klein, you got to let me help. I know guys out of work, they'll come around and protect you. Real protection, for no cost.' You know what he told me? 'Murphy, *you* got the troubles today, not me. So a few kids will come in while we're back here and steal a dozen apples. Is it going to kill anybody? I can't fight it. But today, *you* got the problem because *you* lost your job.' 'I didn't lose it exactly,' I told him. 'It's April. Nobody buys firewood in April.' 'It's still losing your job,' he said. 'Here, take a drink.'

"Here he is, this little guy, I didn't think he even knew what drinking was all about, and he's got a few bottles stashed away. He's got glasses, too, the works. There we are, eleven in the morning, two fancy guys having a drink. And I mean he's got some fancy scotch. Six bucks a bottle, baby. But what I like about him is how he poured me the most, and him the least, and all the time he's wearing this expression like, You didn't think I was the type, did you? Terrific guy. Terrific guy. I loved him like he was my own flesh and blood. I couldn't have loved nobody more. 'Now, be careful,' he says to me. 'Don't think that because we did this you can come here anytime you like and have a free one on the old man.' He was laughing when he said it. You know, I could have stole a bottle from him anytime. He made sure I knew where he kept them. But the way he did it, trusting me like that, there was no way in the world I would have gone behind his back. He trusted me, I wanted to make sure he always would. That's the only way I could repay him. He wanted to call me a mick, that's all right with me 'cause I know he trusts me, not that Klein would ever call me that. Not *that* man. But I could have called him a sheeny, and I know he would have been my friend.

"We saw the world changing together, right through the windows of that little store of his. Each year, you know, I could see his shelves holding less and less stuff. He couldn't keep up with the stock, and he never pretended he could. We saw the world changing. New people moving in, old friends of ours moving out. We could see by how many people came into his store, and who they were, what their color was, how the world was changing. We'd be in there a lot, in the later years, by ourselves, 'cause he was running low on business when the big supermarket went in and wiped him out. They undercut him on every price. All he had to sell was friendship and trust. But people don't want that nowadays. They want the best prices, no matter how they're treated. People go to save three cents, not make a friend, or keep a good friend, like Klein was.

"Funny, I just thought, you know, he spoke with an accent but he told me he was born in this country. I couldn't figure it out. I thought maybe he was lying. A guy lives here all his life and speaks with an accent? I remember one day listening in on him talking with his wife. I figured, okay, now I'll learn what language he really speaks. English. They spoke English. He's bawling her out about something and she's getting even with him, in *English*. That's the amazing part, all these people in the old neighborhood, they spoke English. Sure, you got your Italians who speak Italian, but we're all speaking English. Nobody's a foreigner here, but they're ready to kill each other. People will go after anybody. You don't think the Jews went after each other? You should have seen the arguments I heard in those years. *They* fought, *we* fought, the Poles fought, the Italians. We all could have killed each other, our own kind, anybody's kind. You take a swing, you catch a swing. *That's* the *real* international language, like they say. But old Klein, he was never a part of it. I wept the day they opened that supermarket. He went to see it. Apron and all, he wanted to see it for himself. I told him, 'It's a monster, I hate it.' 'It's no monster,' he said, 'it's progress. You think businesses like *this* have a future?' Each day, no kidding, each day his shelves got emptier and emptier. It go so I hated to go in there I felt so bad for the guy.

"I'd tell him, 'Klein, the world changes, supermarkets, big housing projects. What happens to the little ethnic grocery store?' He loved hearing me talk like that. 'Ethnic,' he'd say, 'what's so ethnic about this place? It's a little store with a shrinking stock.' He knew he was headed out, and I'm talking when he was over seventy. He looked his age, past his age, too. He was always tired and old-looking. The two of them put in twelve hours a day. I used to figure out what they made an hour because occasionally he'd let me help him close up and I'd count the money in the register. He called it the box. 'Enough in the box,' he'd say 'in case we're robbed. They shouldn't get disappointed when they find so little. Crooks, they get angry when they find out that not everybody who runs a grocery store is a millionaire.' Jesus, I could have cried when he talked that way. Millionaire? The absolute tops that man made in a day, I mean, he couldn't have cleared thirty, forty bucks. And he was there, with his wife, seven days a week. 'Where your children?' I asked him once. 'Cause I saw he had pictures all over the place. 'How come they don't help?' He looked at me and laughed. He said, 'We taught them to study hard and be smart. They did. They are. What do they want to come around here for? They tell us, sell. Sell to who? To what? You want to buy this place, Murphy?' I was embarrassed. I couldn't even answer. 'Of course, you don't want it. Who in his right mind would want it? Only the guy that has it, right? You heard of a white elephant, Murphy? This one's pink!'

"Guy had a sense of humor on him. You had to, to stay there like he did. His problem, see, was that he believed in people. He believed if he was kind, people would be kind. So the people ate him up. They stole his stock, they robbed him blind. This one time he was robbed, it was in the neighborhood paper. I was reading, sitting in his own store.

" 'Hey, Klein, what's this?' I told him. 'You were robbed but you never told me.' 'What's to tell?' he said. I said, 'What's to *tell*? Are you crazy? Did you report this to the cops?' Sure, he reported it to the cops. 'So what are they going to do about it?' 'Well, they'll look into it, I don't know.' 'Don't you even want to talk about it?' I asked. I mean, sometimes I thought the guy was a little too much on the weak, let's-not-talk-about-it side. But this time he was doing it for *me*. I said, 'What the hell's going on here? I'm going to talk with your wife.' 'She doesn't know nothing about it,' he says. I says, 'What is it with you?' And he's just staring at me. So it comes to me: They're Irish guys that robbed him and he doesn't want to start trouble or make me think something bad. So I told him, 'I swear to God, Klein, I'd beat the living Jesus out of my own mother if I thought she took a penny off you. My own mother.' 'You couldn't handle your own mother,' he said. 'Come on, I got some new scotch,' which he did have, too. That's some kind of a guy to do that. I had my scotch and I went right away to the police and told them about Klein knowing who robbed him. So the cop tells me, 'Klein knows exactly who it was. He saw all three of the men but he's afraid to say nothing 'cause he's sure they got friends who'll come for him again.' Of course, that's what would happen. In that neighborhood? That's exactly what would happen, too. Not in the old days, though.

"Klein used to say it himself: 'We all depend on one another,' he'd say. 'You don't depend on laws. You depend on people being good. You take, like, I walk down the sidewalk, how do I know a guy isn't going to drive up and wipe me out? 'Cause there's a law that says he can't do that? Maybe he's drunk. Maybe he has a heart attack. You just believe it will be all right. If you worried about all these things, you wouldn't move out of a hole in the ground.' That's the way he lived, that's the way we all live. Then the times change, and now you can't trust anyone about anything. Drive up on the curb to hit you? They'll come into your house and rob you even if you're ninety years old. You think they had respect for him? Maybe they cared he was a Jew? Some of 'em nowadays are such animals they don't even know what a Jew *is*. Country falls apart and people beome animals. Eight years old and they're animals. Klein's philosophy went, trust them, it's the only way. He used to say, 'Lucky for him he was old and poor. He had nothing to lose.' I told him, in the old days he could be sure to live a long time. Now anybody who promised him anything was a fool. He knew all about this. He told me, live life minute by minute, the days go fast enough. You know, he was like a teacher. I learned more from that man than I ever learned in the schools I went to. I think Jews are a little smarter than most of us about how to live. They've never had it too easy. Look, here, at his case. What did he want from life? To have a few regular customers, that's all. The new supermarket could go on, that was fine. Just a few of his old standbys could have stayed around. But they didn't. The neighborhood went to hell, and when it went, I mean it went fast. They got out. We all got out. Klein, though, he didn't get out.

"Now, this part of the story is where I get mad. The fire comes and the man and his wife are caught in it and they perish. Their bodies were recovered and identified. They died in that fire, everybody knew it. It was in the papers. But because they were Jewish, and people knew how tough it was for them, everybody said they set fire to their own store to collect insurance, only something went wrong and they died. I personally had arguments with ten people. 'Murphy, you can't see the truth. Jews are always a little trickier with money. The old man knew he was on the way out, and he figured he'll get something out of the place. He couldn't get back the blood, sweat, and tears, but he'd get a few dollars out of that crummy neighborhood. Jews do it like that, Murphy. That's the way they operate. Nothing against them, but they're clever. We could take a few lessons from them.' I almost hit the guy. I would have but I had the old lady with me. They aren't tricky, and Klein wasn't tricky. He was a good guy. What the hell did he ever have? His family? That store? He had nothing, and the little he had he gave away, like all that scotch. Didn't he give me a bottle at Christmas every year? Wrapped up, and Jews, they don't celebrate Christmas. I got him Christmas presents but he didn't celebrate it. Do it for the insurance, my Irish blue eye. Kill himself by mistake? He never made a mistake in his life, Klein. He misjudged because he wanted things to be better, but those ain't mistakes.

"All this happened, see, after we moved away. I hadn't seen him for a number of months. First, I saw the fire on television one night and I thought, it's the old neighborhood. Then I saw the cleaning shop next door, 'cause the whole store was gone, and I said, Oh my sweet Lord, it's him. Then I read he and his wife died. I wanted to go to the funeral but I didn't know, would there even be a funeral, 'cause there was nothing mentioned in the papers. I looked in all of them. Klein, Klein, Klein, no Klein. Then I thought, maybe they wouldn't let non-Jews in even if there was a funeral, but I thought, they gotta. I went back to the old neighborhood, walked around. Went to the old guy in the cleaning store, but he sold out. Went to the pharmacy, but that guy wasn't around anymore, though his partner was. I even went to talk to the police. Nothing. Nobody knew. Mr. and Mrs. Klein, as far as everybody I talked to was concerned, were vanished off the face of the earth. No good-byes, no services, nothing. Nobody knew when he came to the neighborhood, nobody knew where he was. All of this is happening in three, four weeks, 'cause I got down there as soon as I could. That's the least I could do for the guy.

"So finally my wife, who sees I'm really shook up by this horrible accident, and I'm convinced it *is* an accident no matter what these stiffs tell me, she says, 'You got to give up, John. You have to let go of Klein who's your last connection to the old neighborhood.' I hadn't seen it that way. I was still attached to something back there. It wasn't my old house, or the old bar, or where my friends lived; it was Klein, and I didn't even know his first name. A Jew was my last connection to the place, and I had to give it all up once and for all. She was right. Except for one thing. Did Klein do it for the insurance and make a mistake, or was it like I wanted it to be, a horrible, horrible accident?

Changing Neighborhoods: Johnnie Murphy and Mr. Klein

"I didn't tell my wife nothing, I just started making my own little investigations. I was working then, so I had to do it on Saturdays, and make sure nobody would catch on to what I was doing. Like a private eye. Hell, I talked to everybody in the neighborhood, at the police, the city hall. If I talked to one lawyer I talked to fifty. I even talked to Klein's son at one point there. He seemed like a nice enough guy. In the end it came out just like I thought. Klein set fire to his shop for the insurance? If he did, he was pretty stupid because he canceled his fire insurance five years before the accident. He set fire to his own store like I discovered America. I told this to all these wise guys with their remarks about how clever Jews are with money. Clever guys don't burn themselves up. Klein's son told me he inherited bills from his father. *Bills*. Klein never had no money. He paid his rent, bought his groceries from his own stock. They had no clothes. He wore the same shoes every day. Set fire for the insurance, my Irish eye. I told this to these guys. They were surprised, a little sad, too, like me, although I don't think none of 'em care all that much for human life. Maybe they don't like Jews. They're like everybody else. Go where they can save a few pennies, forget about real friendships. I learned from that old man. Just getting old don't make nobody smart. You got to meet a man like Klein, he'll teach you what smart is. Man changed my feeling about a lot of things. I'm glad I didn't go to his funeral. I would have cried like a baby.

"I heard a rumor that somebody burned his store down. Maybe they didn't know the old couple was inside. Fireman told me they was suspecting arson, but they didn't want to spread the information around. This way, you don't have people on Klein's side going out looking for revenge. That's modern times for you, isn't it? That's what Klein called progress. Didn't he tell me a hundred times, what's the use of calling the cops? I think someone burned the place down. I ain't saying who. So goddamn many people hating one another these days. Every day someone else gets it. They're animals.

96

Changing Neighborhoods: Johnnie Murphy and Mr. Klein

"Klein was so poor he took to living in the store because he couldn't pay the rent on the store and his own home. He didn't tell nobody because he was ashamed. His own son didn't know. He had no phone, only at the store. Mattresses on the floor, a dirty toilet, I saw it. Maybe he was even living there when I was visiting him. Maybe when we locked up the place he'd walk around and come right back and let himself in. But it was dangerous living there. Those places got broken into at night. And here you got these two elderly people sleeping on mattresses on the floor. They had no room there. You could barely sit down the place was so crowded. They were like animals, different kind of animals from the people who robbed from them, but like I say, living like animals.

"There's another possibility, too. Maybe they did burn the old place down themselves, but not for the insurance. Maybe they decided it's too hard. When I found out about the insurance, I told this to my wife. She told me, 'No way Jewish people commit suicide.' I said, 'What the hell you talking about, Jewish people don't commit suicide?' 'It's against their religion,' she says. I said, 'It may be against their religion, but when you're nothing but an animal and you got dignity like Klein had dignity, maybe you decide, the hell with religion, I can't take it no more. They're also poor people,' I told her. 'They're not *only* Jewish people.'

"So you know what I did? I went to the Jewish temple and talked to the rabbi. I told him I was a Catholic but I wanted to speak to him about a Jewish friend. I wouldn't tell him Klein's name, because if Klein did commit suicide, I wanted, like, to protect his memory. The rabbi said I was right; Jewish people commit suicide. When they're beaten down, they do it. 'Jews are human, too.' That's what he said. I told him after knowing this old man, I thought maybe some Jewish people were more than human. I couldn't say it exactly right, but something like that. The rabbi, young fellow, didn't look like I thought he would. He said, 'No. Jews are just human, and that's a lot.' I told him okay, but I said to myself, if I want to think Klein was special, I'll keep thinking he's special. And I'll stop calling him Klein and call him Mr. Klein as I should have done all along, although he never would have gone along with it. Lucky I didn't go to his funeral. I would have cried like a baby."

Johnnie Murphy turned his head. He looked down the long wall of the bar. Then he studied the empty beer glass before him. His light blue eyes were moist. He said one more thing before getting up to leave.

"Man taught me so much, and I never got around to thanking him. You learn so much from people like that and you never tell 'em how you feel. You fight with people who talk against him, but to the man himself you don't say a word. God damn it!"

Five

Witnesses: Anna Leibovitz, Willy Goldman, Sonny Blitstein, Rose Orlovsky

What some of us call bitching and moaning is captured in the Yiddish word *kvetching*. A *kvetch* is someone who is always complaining, always finding fault with something or someone. No one alive in the areas where the Jewish poor, where all the poor live, could be anything but a *kvetch*. Indeed, family advocates, community leaders, protectors of individual and collective rights of these people must all be *kvetches*, but only up to a point. Beyond a certain point, no one listens to the *kvetch*, for what he or she will do or say becomes predictable. "Do something about it and stop *kvetching*," comes the advice. "It does no good to *kvetch*." Some people, learning this lesson well, never *kvetch*, never raise their voice against social evils, the oppressions of poverty, the dehumanizing and ultimately killing nature of normal social routines and ceremonies. They rarely complain, minimize their own personal situation, the destiny that has brought them this far, and say publicly, and possibly privately as well, that they are thankful to be where they are and to have lived as long as they have. It could be worse, these people say. It could be worse: It *was* worse once, which means it must be better now.

So accepting who they are and what they have been and become, they have learned not to publicize their feelings, their bitterness and rage, their hopelessness and dismay. In conversation, as in the day-by-day leading of their life, they try not to impose upon or burden others with their own personal hurts and wants. They feel that silence may be the best gift they can offer to those near them, who, like them, live in a world where safety, security, and calm are strangers.

But the feelings, memories, and wishes remain, too strong to be permanently ignored. Despite the strongest will, they erupt in the form of fragments, testimonies, stories, like the four that follow. As long as such stories are told, there is hope. Or so we would believe.

Anna Karansky was born in a small Polish town outside of Warsaw. Her parents, both of them farm workers, moved into the Warsaw Ghetto in the mid-1930s when they found it difficult to earn a living off the soil. Anna's father worked in a shoe repair shop, her mother, when not immersed in raising two sons and two daughters, took occasional jobs with a tailor. Most of her work was done at home in the evenings.

By the mid-1930s Shimon Leibovitz, a handsome Ghetto resident and neighbor of the Karanskys, had made two decisions. First he was going to marry the beautiful Anna Karansky no matter what her parents said. Second, he was going to take her out of Poland; it didn't matter where. War seemed near and anti-Semitism was frighteningly apparent.

Shimon and Anna were married in Warsaw in 1936 and left for the United States exactly one year later, eventually settling in Boston. Despite their efforts and the efforts of cousins from the Ghetto who also immigrated to America, the Leibovitzes were unable to get their many relatives out of Poland. Their immediate families and an untold number of cousins, aunts, and uncles died in concentration camps.

I wasn't really surprised when Mrs. Anna Leibovitz suggested one September afternoon that we go to the baseball game. Anyone who meets her learns quickly of her interest in the game and her deep concern for the destiny of the Boston Red Sox. If one visits her at the bakery she runs on Clyer Street in the Jamaica Plain section of Boston or at her small apartment ten blocks away on Wellington Avenue on an afternoon or evening the Red Sox are playing, one will find her listening to the game. At sixty-eight Anna Leibovitz considers herself as loyal a baseball fan as anyone in this country, even though she spent the first half of her life in Poland.

And so we sat together in the right-field bleachers of Fenway Park on a beautiful autumn afternoon. The crowd was small and the distance from our seats to home plate seemed so great I wondered whether Anna could even see the ball leave the pitcher's hand, or follow it after it had been hit, but she saw everything. Between pitches, and especially between innings when one enjoys one of baseball's omnipresent lulls, I saw Anna Leibovitz thinking, sorting through memories she might wish to tell me. She knew well the incongruity I saw in her interest in baseball.

A short woman with smooth white skin, her forehead dotted with specks of brown, her nose straight, turning up just slightly at the end, and her gray-blue eyes always so misty, teary even when she fetches memories for me, she loves looking out on the beautiful green outfield and breathing the air of the bleachers, even if it is filled with the odor of peanuts and beer. "Only in America," she said. "This is what you stay alive for.

People yelling, having a good time, getting a little drunk, but nobody hurting nobody. Nobody's in danger out here, except if Mr. Yastrzemski socks it out this way and you're not ready for him." Anna smiled at me and rubbed her forearm as if she were chilled. "That's why I don't come here alone. When something flies over the wall, somebody big like you should be sitting here ready to catch it. Anna watches the Red Sox, Anna doesn't catch the ball. A dollar and a half for one of these seats, that's a fair enough price. But for these prices they can't expect me to catch the ball. Now," she announced as Rico Petrocelli stepped into the batter's box almost four hundred feet away, "Petrocelli is going to do it for us. I'm predicting. Hit it, Rico," she said, making no effort to yell, "It wouldn't kill you. You might even like it."

On the first pitch Petrocelli lined a shot down the left-field line that went over the wall fifty feet foul. Anna shook her head as the men around us swore at the Boston third baseman. I heard her say, "Poor Mr. Petrocelli. Maybe they should try glasses on him, give him something to drink. All he does is hits home runs on the wrong side. One time it's too far this way, one time too far that way, maybe he should stand different. Then when he hits it, it's coming here." She paused, reflecting on her own words. "Ach, maybe he's just not strong enough. They say he's got temperament. That'll get you into trouble. You can't be that way and play this game."

A peculiar look came over Anna's face, breaking her concentration and causing her eyes to close slightly.

"What is it?" I asked.

"My cousin Sylvio was nineteen years old when the Germans killed him. Big shot. He was one of the big shots. Nineteen years old standing in the doorway of an apartment house, what we'd call a town house. Big brown door, twice his size, I remember. Jews, many of them living in there, none of them related to any of us. This was in Wocawek, I think. Who remembers now? Who wants to remember these things? I don't

even know if there were any Jews at all there, in Wocawek.
Maybe it was Radam. Anyway, Sylvio with the temperament,
he's going to be Mr. Big, protecting everybody. So he stands
there in the doorway and this young German officer asks to go
inside but Sylvio tells him no. Just like that. A big shot. The
officer wants to go inside. Sylvio says no. So the officer asks
again, and Sylvio says no. You can guess what happened."

"They shot him?"

"Only five times," Anna answered with no emotion in her
voice but her lips pursed. "And here's Mr. Petrocelli, striking
out. That doesn't help," she groaned. "You see what that
temperament gets you. It gets you three pitches and all you can
hit is a home run in the wrong direction. So now comes Mr.
Griffin, who I always call Merv because he has a first name I
can't remember if they told it to me fifty times."

"Doug Griffin," I helped her.

"Doug Griffin. Such an uninteresting name. Maybe
second-base players have uninteresting names. Not shortstops.
Luis Aparicio," she said with obvious relish.

"You like that name, huh?"

"Sure, it's Polish, isn't it?" Anna began laughing as did a
man behind us who had overheard her.

"You tell 'em, mother. Aparicio's a Polack, all right."

Anna turned around and waved her finger at the man,
who was beet red from sitting in the sun. "Not a Polack, a Pole.
Just a Pole." Anna looked at me and grinned. "So Aparicio's not
a Pole. Who can tell from out here? He could be a Pole.
Everybody Polish in Boston has his real name? Your friend
Griffin could be Gratovsky, huh? Carleton Fisk, that's his real
name? A Pole!"

"Anna, your cousin Sylvio, did he have an option?"

"Option?"

"Could he have done something else?"

"Sure, he could have turned away, let the officer into the
building, and got shot in the back with five bullets instead of in

the front. A lot of the resistance in those days, you know, was young people. Fifteen, sixteen, young, all of them. They knew they didn't have a chance against the Nazis but they fought, they made trouble. They watched their mothers and fathers and sisters get killed, taken to the camps, so they hid as long as they could and did what they could. Out here Yastrzemski, Petrocelli, your friend Carleton Fisk are heroes. Only when they lost, they didn't play anymore like those nogoodniks."

Anna hadn't missed a pitch. When the Red Sox went out in order, she opened the program and studied the photos of the ballplayers. I imagined her trying to recall the faces of her relatives and friends who perished in Eastern Europe when she was a young woman. None of her friends in this country had ever heard the details of Anna and Shimon Leibovitz's escape from Poland. They knew only that the Leibovitzes landed in Baltimore and made their way first to New York, then to Boston. By listening to the immigrant couple they learned that the years in America had been good ones. A bakery business established by Shimon's cousin, Walter Wilensky, who had immigrated six months before the Leibovitzes, had done rather well. The Leibovitzes were quick to say they were never rich, but they were also far from poor. Walter had gotten married and had two children, both of whom had gone to college. The Leibovitzes never had children, but they watched the Wilensky children grow up as if they were their own.

"What are you thinking, Anna?"

Anna didn't look up from the program. "I'm thinking that lots of these boys here look too young to be making so much money. We could have used some of that money. Not for me, but my poor Shimon." She sighed. "He always told people he had no complaints, that he was glad just to be alive with something to eat, but he wanted to have more. I knew it. He wanted the feeling of having real money. What we went through, you know, was frightening. Everybody knows. But it was"—she struggled for the word—"you come out of it ashamed. The whole world could think we were right and the Germans were wrong. Everybody could be on our side, but what they did makes you feel small. You walk around like you had a smear on your face and people are afraid to tell you how you look. Shimon always was ashamed. Still, we had a lot of happy years here."

"Would you go back, to visit? Would you like that?"

Anna looked up from her program just in time to see Boog Powell of the Orioles come to the plate. "Who's this?" she asked. "Somebody new?"

"Powell."

"A big man. He's hitting for somebody?"

"He's pinch-hitting."

"Such a word, pinch-hitting. Visit Poland? No." Her tone was stern. "I'll never go back to Europe. It's not the money. That part of my life is over. It had good parts, too. Very lovely parts, very lovely occasions. I was born there, my parents died there, I met my husband there, but all of it is gone. Now I'm here, this is my country," she said, gesturing toward the grandstands and playing field. "You know, people are strong, they come through things. Sometimes at night you think over your life, maybe you dream a little, maybe you dream a little too much even." Anna smiled. "Maybe you cry a little too because nobody sees. But people live through it. The lucky ones, they live through. And you start all over again, almost brand-new. I have my job, I have my home, I have friends like you, I have my Red Sox, my special boyfriends, Petrocelli and Carleton Fisk, and Mr. Aparicio, and that makes for a good life. This is peace out here for me, people yelling, shouting, kill the umpire, kill this one, kill that one, people hoping, screaming. It's wonderful. Baseball's wonderful, America's wonderful. The noise is wonderful. It's at night when it's quiet and you're lying in the bed and you can't sleep because it's so quiet, that's when I worry. There could be a knock on the door. A dog could be barking that you're not sure why he's barking, there can be a sound. But out here, everybody makes noise and nobody gets hurt. That's when I feel peaceful."

Boog Powell had lifted a long high fly which had taken Boston's right fielder to the warning track.

"He'll catch it," Anna was saying confidently. "Don't worry, he'll catch it. If he doesn't have to run, he'll catch it. It's when he runs that he doesn't do so good."

As predicted, Reggie Smith caught the ball and Anna squinted in the sun at the next batter who walked slowly to the plate that seemed a hundred miles away.

"You know," she remarked, "as the game goes on the players get smaller. Could it be that I'm getting tired sitting in the sun? It could be. Brooks Robinson. This is a ballplayer."

Anna adjusted her position on the hard bleacher bench. She looked quickly behind her but the men were concentrating on the game. "I'll tell you something else. When you get old, and you come from what I came from, people look at you and feel sorry, or they think you're doing pretty good for an old lady, or they're pleased that you got a little money and a clean apartment, that you don't have to worry. But I don't think about that so much. I think about the future. Maybe I could travel a little in America. I have relatives in Chicago I write to. Maybe I'll visit them. Maybe I could go to Florida again when it gets cold, maybe I'll fix my apartment. I still have plans, lots of things to do." She grinned. "I'd drop them all for the baseball game."

"You suggesting I should invite you again?" I teased.

"From the middle of work I'll run out here. They play so much at night. How can people like me come here at night? I got a friend, maybe she's a cousin, from Częstochowa. You know where that is, Częstochowa?"

"No."

"No matter. She lives now in Cincinnati. You know where Cincinnati is?"

I laughed.

"I told her, how can I come to Cincinnati and see you? She writes back, I'll get you a ticket. I write back, what good is a ticket going to do me? The Red Sox don't go to Cincinnati. I go where they go. I looked on the map. You want me to visit, I wrote her, you'll move either to Cleveland or Detroit, then I'll visit. And I'll bring Mr. Yastrzemski and Mr. Petrocelli and Mr. Luis Aparicio and all my other American friends and we'll sit in the bleachers and we'll scream and enjoy ourselves and thank God we can have a good time.

"So you know what she says? She writes back, if that's the way you feel, don't come. I'm not moving to please you. Besides, if Mr. Johnny Bench isn't good enough for you, then stay home with all your Boston snob friends. How do you like that? Boston snob friends. So I wrote her, what does she mean Boston's so snobby? What's she upset about? 'Cause there's nothing to be snobby about in Cincinnati except Johnny Bench? I like it better here with my Carleton Fisk." Anna shrugged, and for an instant a serious look covered her face. Then she shook her head. "Is that his real name, you think? Carleton Fisk? It couldn't be something like, like Sylvio Fisk?"

Willy Goldman, Sam Dickstein, Benny Meltzer, Harry Berman, and Abe Fleishman were all Boston boys. Born in Boston, raised in Boston, schooled in Boston, first jobs in Boston, Boston was their lifeblood. Willy was the son of Esther and Harry Goldman, whose name wasn't Goldman at all. Emigrés from Russia, the couple had traveled for years throughout Eastern Europe, barely eking out a living. Finally they were able to secure passage to the United States, landing in South Carolina. It was here that they chose the name Goldman, and rented an apartment.

The year was 1890. Work was hard to come by, as the

couple had expected. In an attempt to find employment, they were obliged to settle in several cities on a trial basis, among them Baltimore, Richmond, Philadelphia, New York, and Orlando. Boston finally won out.

Unlike his parents, Willy never experienced the constant uprootings. He was Massachusetts through and through.

Strange, how when a man like Willy Goldman dies, everybody seems to come out of the woodwork claiming they knew him intimately, perhaps even grew up with him. Benny Meltzer did just that, telling anyone who would listen that "Willy Goldman was a beautiful man. He was a beautiful man from the time he was ten years old—and don't think I can't remember him then—to the instant he took his last breath. *Alava sholem*. How old was he, Sam?"

Sam Dickstein was Willy Goldman's cousin on his mother's side. He never liked Benny Meltzer. What is more, he well knew that Willy shared his feeling, referring to Benny as a walking pickle. But when people are sitting shiva in a small, crowded Brighton apartment and everyone including myself has come to pay his respects, maybe weep a little, reminisce, and probably worry about when it's going to be his own time, it's no time to dwell on hatreds.

"Willy Goldman was fifty-seven last June, my friend. Not old. Not old at all," Sam sighed. His large brown eyes looked tired. "You don't believe these things. You remember, Harry," he said, turning to Harry Berman, who thirty-five years ago married Willy Goldman's sister, although they might just as well have been born married, since no one remembers their being more than three feet apart. "You remember, Harry," Sam Dickstein continued, "when Willy and me and you and that *pasgoodnik* Fleishman, Abe Fleishman, you remember him?"

Harry nodded and allowed himself to smile. "Abe

Fleishman," he recalled slowly, "took my sister on a canoe trip somewhere up in Maine, my parents didn't even know, and he's taking her there like he's some big-shot canoe expert, and he's never been in a boat before and he falls in and almost drowns. *She* pulls him out. Four feet three, and she's pulling him out of this freezing cold lake up in Maine. Do I remember Abe *Fleish*man? Do *you* remember, watch this now," he bumped Benny Meltzer on the arm. "Do you remember Sankowitz who used to sell those *pishocka* toys in South Station? On the floor with the boxes?"

"Do I remember Sankowitz?" Sam replied. "Mr. Memory Man here is asking, do I remember Sankowitz. First of all, his name wasn't Sankowitz, it was Sankowsky with a 'y.' And his first name was something no one ever knew because no one could say it anyway, and so this Yiddle they called, are you ready, Salvatore."

"*Oi*, how this man remembers," Harry muttered.

"How he remembers," Sam mocked his good friend. "Who the hell gave Sankowsky his start? Who had the pharmacy going in the station all those years? That *mamzer* stole everything from me. I used to go to Hartford with Sonny Mannister, you remember Sonny Mannister?"

Suddenly Benny Meltzer joined in. "I knew Sonny very well," he blurted out. "Sonny grew up, Sonny grew up, where the hell did he live in those days?"

"On Clinton Boulevard with every other kike and nogoodnik in the city." Sam was laughing out loud.

Harry was embarrassed and began looking around at the others in the room. "*Oi*, do you remember Clinton Boulevard, how it used to freeze there?" Harry was covering his eyes and shaking his head.

"In the winter it froze," Sam said flatly. "In the summer it didn't. Willy Goldman used to live, I'll tell you exactly. Willy Goldman lived," his words were coming slowly, "at 1132, which I know because *his* father and *my* father lived together a few months after my grandmother died at 1151, which was right across the street, and that was above Klapstein's Pharmacy. You remember Klapstein?" Sam turned to Harry.

"Did I clean floors in Klapstein's?" Harry responded dutifully.

"*You* washed floors in Klapstein's, Harry?" Sam was shaking his head in disbelief. "So how come I don't remember that? I was in that store every day of my life and what am I three, four years older than you? Where the hell *were* you?"

"How old are you?" Harry asked pointedly.

"I'll be fifty-eight in November," Sam answered. "I'm Goldman's year. 1915."

"Jesus, he doesn't look it," Benny Meltzer said. "Does he look it? You don't look any fifty-seven, Sam. Honest to God."

"He looked fifty-seven when he was eighteen years old," Harry chided Sam.

"Stinker!" Sam shouted at Harry. "Where were you sweeping in that store? Klapstein's. Why didn't I see you? I had perfect eyes all my life."

"Because you were so busy stealing from the old man Klapstein you never looked down to see who was wiping the floor, that's why."

"You know, I swear to God," Sam said, raising his right hand, "I absolutely can't remember seeing this guy in that place in, Jesus, it must have been at least ten years I went in there almost every day. How old are you, Harry? You're my age, right? What are you, sixty? You're older, no?"

"Take a guess." Harry Berman thrust his face first at Sam, then at Benny. He looked excited.

"I wouldn't put you a day past fifty-five," Benny said promptly, perhaps hoping to get into Harry's good graces.

"Take that ugly *punim* out of my face," Sam barked at his friend. "Fifty-five? He's closer to sixty-five, for Chrissakes. What the hell, you were out of high school in 1928. I got married in '38."

"Is he right, Harry?" Benny asked.

"Shh, let him figure it out. Go on, figure it out, Sammy," he challenged his friend.

Sam Dickstein stroked his jaw and scanned Harry's body. For a full minute he studied his friend and listened to the others talking softly in the room. At last he spoke. "How the hell could I have not known you worked at Klapstein's, and what the hell do you mean I *stole* from him? I never touched a thing in that store."

"You never touched a thing," Harry snickered. "Sure you never touched a thing. You were too busy putting it in your mouth. You never touched . . ."

"Oh, *candy*," Sam said with relief. "Sure I took candy. I took it every day for ten years. I bet I stole a box of that *chazarai* a day when I was a kid. Every kid did it. What's the big deal?"

"So you *did* steal, like I told you. So I saw you. That's all. I rest my case."

"Sure you saw me. But it was candy. Who could care about candy? I thought you meant I stole perfume or medicine or something important. Who the hell had enough food in those days? I took candy for survival. Nobody ever called that stealing."

"You could have got arrested," Benny intervened mildly.

"I could have got arrested?" Sam was nodding to Benny as if to say, you're a *pisher*, Meltzer. I'm doing you a favor just listening to your voice and putting up with the fact that you're standing here. If it weren't so soon after poor Willy's death, I'd really tell you something about getting arrested. For Chrissakes, if Goldman knew you were here acting like you were a close friend, he'd turn over three times in that *choloschus* casket his wife bought from God only knows who. From Pincus probably, the *ganif* who goes around with that smart-ass smile of his hoping we'll all *pager* so he can cry in that phony way and sell somebody another casket for two grand or whatever the hell he soaks you for it.

"You remember, Harry, when we got arrested, Willy and me and that, what was his name—Kinky, Konky something? At Redmonds in Jamaica Plain?"

"Not at Redmonds," Sam said firmly. "In Cambridge after that dance, when we broke into that warehouse where the cops were playing cards. Jesus. And this, this guy, ah, Kinky, Konky, what the hell was his name? Masserman? Something like that. Masserman, I think. The kid dives through the window with a goddamn corned beef sandwich in one hand and a bottle of something, Jesus, I think it was ninety-eight percent proof in the other, and lands right in the middle of this card game the cops are having there. Kinky, Konky something. Right in the cops' laps, and we're flying in, a couple of George Rafts right after him. You remember that, Harry? You were with us. That has to go back a hundred years." He waved his hands in the air as if he were giving up trying to figure out anything anymore.

"Sure I remember," Harry answered. It was evident that he didn't.

"Kingy Masserman." Sam had remembered the name. "Kingy Masserman, with the corned beef in one hand and the ninety-eight proof in the other, and we were drunk," his voice rose. "*Gutinu*, were we drunk."

"So they arrested you?" Benny prodded Sam.

"These cops there, they grabbed us by the collar and dragged us to the station, must have been on McDermott and Chelsea. Three big Irish guys, I remember. I still see one of them. He works around here. Used to be over in Mattapan. Big guy. So they ask us, 'You got a lawyer?' Three Clarence Darrows sitting there, Masserman's still got the sandwich, I'm ready to cry, Goldman's looking like if his father finds out where he is, he's going to chop off his *putz* with a knife right there in the precinct."

Harry and Benny were convulsed.

"Do we have a lawyer, this guy wants to know. Sure, we

got Clarence Darrow. Who else? You remember what we did?" Sam asked Harry.

Harry nodded obligingly, obviously not remembering the story in the slightest.

"We called Elaine Fishman, right? Elaine Fishman was the most beautiful girl in Brighton. There wasn't a Yiddle in Massachusetts didn't know Elaine Fishman. 'Member how they were going to put her up for Miss America, Miss Massachusetts or something, until they found out she was Jewish?" Sam was looking around the room again, incredulous at his own memories. "How all of this comes back to you," he mumbled. "What does it do all this time, just sit there in your head?"

"Elaine Fishman," Harry reminded him.

"Oh, so we call up Fishman and tell her what's happened and where we are, see. Willy did it because she liked him. I'll bet she doesn't even know about this," he interrupted himself, recalling the events of the last couple of days. "We know, see, that if it's late at night, Elaine Fishman's got to be on a couch with some guy, right? But not just any guy. Some smart guy, a rich guy, someone who maybe before they started doing what they were doing at four o'clock in the morning was all dressed up. You know what I mean? Earlier that night," Sam explained, pushing his finger in the air, "he'd looked mature. So Willie asks her, 'Who you with? What are you doing? She says, 'It's none of your goddamn business and it's Fred Weinrod.' " Benny and Harry were smirking. " 'Fred Weinrod. That's perfect. Tell him he's got to get over here right away and pretend he's a lawyer so he can get us out of jail.' So she says, 'He's seventeen years old and he's not wearing a suit, how can he be a lawyer?' 'Send him!!' Willy says. 'Will you listen to me. Get him dressed and send him.'

"So we're waiting with the sandwich and the alcohol, and the police are looking at us like we're *meshuga*, except you can tell that they know we're probably not bad guys. And does this guy come, this Weinrod with his pimples and this kinky hair of his. A schnook from I don't know where. He walks in, and we see he's left Elaine outside, and he walks up to this Irish cop and says he's Mister Somebody or Other, a lawyer naturally, and he's come to get us out. All of a sudden this schnook's having a good time and we don't know whether to laugh or cry. Mr. Pimples is getting us out of there. And the cop is saying, 'Okay, lawyer, take 'em out of here.' So he's done it. And we get out of there, still with the sandwich, and we're outside. We can't believe it's so easy, and the cop comes outside and stands in the door. I can still see him. He's looking at the five of us and we're standing there like children. We don't even know how we're going to get home, and he says real loud, 'You know something, you're *all* of you full of shit!' Jesus, did we run from there! Did we run! Like track stars."

Sam, Harry, and Benny, doubled over with laughter, were receiving, along with me, disapproving looks from others in the room. In spite of the somber setting, they could not put out of their minds the image of Willy Goldman and his friends running scared but relieved through the dark streets of Cambridge toward their homes in Mattapan miles away. But what about the other, darker image, the picture of Willy dying the day before yesterday? What makes a man weave a bunch of ties together and hang himself? A Jewish man. Was he that discouraged, as his note said, that humiliated by failure in his business and in his life, that preoccupied with the feeling that he had let his family and his religion down? And what about his son Jack? Why did the young man throw himself on his father's body after the police had cut it down and laid it out on the cement floor in the basement and cry and say he was sorry, and that it was all his fault that his father killed himself? What would Bess do now? Where does a widow get the strength to go on? Is this the way it happens? Is this what it comes to, all those years?

Nobody could be more American than Sonny Blitstein. In fact, he is so American he never bothers to tell people he was born in Latvia. They would never believe him, he says. Why discuss the trip through Europe to northern France, the boat ride to Boston in the winter of 1914, the horse and cart ride from the dock to Dorchester, where his family would move in with his mother's sister, who had come to America four years earlier? Who cares about my family history? Sonny Blitstein would say. Why burden people with stories of how the little Dorchester apartment, which could barely house the five people in his aunt's family, now somehow contain Sonny's parents and four brothers and sisters as well. Why burden people with stories of the deaths of people, the freezing cold winters, the summers in which they practically baked, the constant anti-Semitism, the kids' problems in schools, the adults' problems in finding work when one was unskilled and spoke a peculiar foreign tongue? What sense did it make to burden people with such stories? Besides, inasmuch as Sonny was only a year and a half old when he came to America, some people might doubt recollections that Sonny *knew* to be perfectly accurate!

I never realized how much I liked Sonny Blitstein until I didn't see him regularly as I had for almost five years. Every time I visited the neighborhood in Mattapan, I invariably found myself at Bargain Drugs, where Sonny and his two partners, Bennie Brown and Alan Jake Jacobson, always had time for a talk. These talks were always the same, composed of delicious reminiscences. All in their middle sixties, the three pharmacists, who clearly loved each other but rarely had a kind word to say to one another, adored evoking the past, especially Sonny. One day it would be train travel between Boston and New York in the 1940s. They could remember the food, the train menus, the card games that started in Grand Central and were still going when the men got off at the Back Bay Station. Another day it was Sonny telling of the time he wanted to impress a young lady he had picked up in the Biltmore Hotel:

"I had this girl, see, nothing too much, but you know how it is, you want to impress 'em, especially the Christian ones. What's she supposed to know, that I'm a two-bit pharmacist from Boston on a cheap weekend in New York? Better to let her think she's out with some Jewish prince with money burning holes in his money belt. You know what I mean?" A story from Sonny always drew a crowd. On this occasion there were five of us, all men, teasing him, urging him on, repeating his words.

"So I take this woman to the most goyish place you've ever seen, the Rainbow Room, Plaza, somewhere, where they got appearing the Mills Brothers. I'm going back now, maybe thirty-five years."

"So you were married," one of the men shouted out gleefully.

"No, I was single," Sonny replied with the facetious tone he used when he was interrupted. "What are you talking about? I said I'm going back thirty-five years. So how long have I been married?"

"Forty-five years, at least," someone said.

"Okay," Sonny nodded, making his point, "of course I was married. What's the harm? I took the kid to the Rainbow Room, that's all. I didn't do nothing else. What did I know how to do anyway?"

Everybody laughed.

"So I want to impress her. So I go up to one of the Mills Brothers and I tell him, 'Be an angel, do me a favor. When you're up there the next time, dedicate a song to the kid I'm with. Say it's 'cause we're old friends.' So he says, 'Sure, I'll do it. What's your name?' So I told him, 'Sonny Blitstein.' So I go sit down at the table and we're having drinks and she's looking around probably wondering when all the Jewish magic she's heard about is going to appear and this guy from the Mills Brothers stands up and says he's going to sing a song for Sonny Blitstein's girl friend 'cause he's an old friend of Sonny's from Boston. I told him that, too."

"So what'd she do?" All of us were spellbound.

"She looks at me," Sonny went on, "*oi*, she was excited. Was I the hit of the evening. She wanted Jewish magic, I gave her Jewish magic. Thirty hours later I was back in Charlestown filling prescriptions, she was probably telling her friends on a yacht someplace about the Jewish prince who took her to the Rainbow Room or the Plaza or wherever we went, and the Mills Brothers were probably thinking, another day, another *shmuck*."

The crowd at Bargain Drugs disbanded. What would happen to all of us, I thought, if this store ever had any business? How could we talk? Sonny used to think the same thing. "What happens to us, doc," he would always say to me, "if we get successful and can't talk? We'll have to go out of business. I mean, what's more important, making money or making friends?"

Money never seemed to trouble Sonny Blitstein. Or if it did, he never discussed it. What Sonny talked about was Sonny Blitstein, and everyone loved it.

I recall a Sunday morning in the back room of the pharmacy with boxes piled up and merchandise scattered all over the floor. There was Sonny and Jake and Sonny's brother Arnold waiting for me to join them. They had laid out the Sunday morning usual, bagels, lox, cream cheese, onions, and a fifth of Jack Daniel's. The food was untouched, the liquor half consumed. I hadn't even reached for the knife when Sonny began talking:

"I'll tell you the truth, doc, I've done everything in my life. I was in a chorus line once, dressed as a girl. I went to

medical school but I quit. There were a million doctors in my
family but *I* had to quit. I worked on a boat. I used to usher at
the Paramount, used to pal around with Eddie what's-his-face
the singer. He was from the old neighborhood. You know what
I done once, I played golf at a country club that was so exclusive
if they used a Jewish caterer, which they did all the time, they
wouldn't let him deliver. They got someone to deliver for them.
God forbid a Jew should have walked on the carpet in their
clubhouse."

"Up in New Hampshire," Jake said, his mouth full of
food.

"Sure," Sonny nodded, "up there, near the beach somewhere. But I played there. I went to school with this guy
Collins. His father was a cop. He was the caddie master there.
He let me play. He told them my name was Blitz and that I just
came up from Hampton Beach. They treated me like a king."

Sonny took a drink. Arnold was giggling.

"What'd you shoot?" I asked.

"Shoot? In golf? Who knew how to play? I dressed like a
prince and walked all over their beautiful rug in the clubhouse.
You'd need a computer to figure out how much I shot. I don't
think I ever played golf before that day. I ever play golf before,
Arnold?"

Arnold shook his head while the rest of us ate and drank.

"I didn't go there to play golf," Sonny continued. "I went
there to walk with my Jewish feet on that sacred rug of theirs."

On another Sunday morning, again over bagels, lox,
cream cheese, and bourbon, Sonny told me the story of how he
almost broke his hand hitting a Nova Scotian chauffeur. He led
off the story with his familiar words, "I done everything in my
life, doc. Everything.

"I'm going back over forty-five years now. I had a job in
Long Island, near the Hamptons. They didn't let a Jew into
nothing there. Nobody knew who I was. I worked in this
pharmacy with a guy—I haven't thought of him in fifty

years—Gino Calabrizi, kid used to be a linebacker with Penn
State. He knew I was a Yid. We worked in the store together
about a year and a half. Nobody liked him, nobody liked me, so
we got along perfect. So one day, in the summer, this chauffeur
from Halifax, he's in the store reading the newspaper and
suddenly he points to this story in the paper how an Arab killed
a Jew somewhere. Who can remember where?" Sonny
shrugged. "So then he says, 'I like that. For my money they can
kill all those kike bastards.' So I start to tiptoe away. I figure,
what do I want to start something. I'll only lose my job. Jobs
were tough then, too."

None of the other men were paying much attention to
Sonny but it didn't bother him. He was grinning, loving every
minute of his own story.

"So a couple days later I'm walking around in one of these
swank places they got out there—I had a friend when I was a
kid named Irving Flexner. He wasn't much that I can remember now except he used to tell me whenever he wanted to
pass he'd tell people his name was Flexner Irving. So I'm
walking in these places, and, doc, they were beautiful, the best,
and I'm calling myself Flexner Irving. I don't think people
would have appreciated Blitstein Sonny. And there's the chauffeur sitting in the lobby. So I go up to him"—Sonny rose from
his seat, practically choking on his bagel—"and I give him a
shot, wham, right in the chin." Sonny gave an imitation of
landing a punch and breaking his fist. "I thought I broke every
bone in my arm. Nothing. The guy's head didn't even move
and my fingers were turning stiff. So he gets up ready to hit me
but this guy Calabrizi, the linebacker from Penn State, is right
behind me. 'You ever see an Italian stick up for a Jew?' he tells
the chauffeur. The guy sits down and Calabrizi and I walk out
of there like we owned the place. Second we got outside we
rushed for his car and went to the hospital to have my hand
fixed.

"That's forty-five years ago and look how little has

119

changed. The Arabs are still killing the Jews, there are still people like that chauffeur who want the Arabs to kill the Jews, and there's still Italians around to protect bigmouths like me."

Sonny was laughing out loud. The men in the back room nodded their heads as if to say they agreed with him. "That's a long time ago, doc," Sonny was saying. "I was a tough Jew then and I'm a tough one now. Only now the world don't want me no more. First they didn't want me 'cause I was a Jew, now they don't want me because I'm almost seventy years old. Go figure it out. They've always got a way to get rid of you."

After that Sunday morning I didn't see Sonny for several months. I visited the old pharmacy and discovered it was being renovated. Practically overnight, every sign of the old place had gone and a modern new store was emerging. The store closed only one day when they put in the gold carpeting. Then it reopened for business, under new ownership. Sonny, Benny, and Jake had sold out to a firm, I was told. Jake and Benny were going to stay on for a while, but Sonny was retired. It was hard to return to the store now. I missed Sonny and the men who always moved about, fingering every item on the shelves and buying absolutely nothing.

Then one July day, months after Bargain Drugs, now Berg Drugs, had been renovated, I saw Sonny getting out of his car near Wentworth Avenue, a block from the store. I sneaked up behind him and squeezed his arm. He turned around suddenly, his face showing happiness, not fear.

"Hey, doc, how are you?"

"Great, and you?"

"Perfect. What could be bad?"

"You look real good, Sonny." He did, too. Sunburned, his black hair slicked back, casual clothes. "How you feeling?"

"I've seen better times," he chuckled. "How else can it feel at my age. Everything hurts."

"You like not working?"

"I've done everything, doc. I've worked, I've gone without work. I got my Social Security, a little money from the store. I'll make out."

"They give you a party?" I asked.

"A party?" Sonny was genuinely surprised. "For what, for a small-time nothing businessman going out the same way he went in? Everything's changed," he sighed. "Look at this neighborhood. Nothing's here that used to be here. Most of the Jewish families don't even live here no more. You seen the store?"

"Yeah."

"You like it?" he asked. I could tell he despised it. He made sure I could tell.

"I despise it," I answered.

"Me, too. He's Jewish, too, this guy we sold to. A Yiddle from Dorchester. Lives in Newton, I think. But you got to be modern, young. Ain't that it? What do they want with an old cocker like me? So I'm retired. I don't miss it." Sonny was smiling. We both knew he was lying.

"You look great," I repeated, not knowing what to say.

"Tell the truth, doc," Sonny grinned at me, "who do I look like?"

"Look like? Someone I know?"

"Look close. Movie star."

"Ah . . ."

"Look at the ears." Sonny pushed his ears out slightly to enlarge their appearance. My face brightened realizing finally the name he was hunting for. "Do I look like Gable? Huh? A little?"

"My God, you do." There was a resemblance, the dark eyes, the slim moustache, the sleek black hair. We all look like movie stars, I thought. "Clark Gable," I said quietly.

"I knew him," Sonny declared.

"You knew Gable?" I asked incredulously.

"Sure. I was working in this place in New York, selling clothes, must be forty years ago. He used to come in there all the time. Had beautiful women with him. He was a gorgeous guy. People loved him."

"Did you call him Clark?"

"No." Sonny's expression said, Are you crazy? "I called him Mr. Gable."

"Did he know your name?"

"Of course he knew my name. I saw him once, twice a month."

"What'd he call you?" I asked.

"He called me what people called me all my life. "Hey, kid, come here. Hey, Charlie, what's the Jew boy's name over there?' "

"Sonny Blitstein," I whispered.

"It's too late for that," Sonny said. "It's all behind me." He paused, his eyes looking slowly about at the old brick buildings on Wentworth Avenue. Then, whatever it was that had occupied him went away. "So how's it with you, doc? You working hard? Taking care of yourself? The wife, kids . . ."

Isaac Orlovsky is what is called a survivor. His parents perished in a Polish death camp. His own journey to America culminated in 1944 when a boat that he and his brother had sneaked onto docked in New York. The next morning they were on a train to Chicago, where they believed they had an uncle.

When the Nazis rode over Poland, Isaac and Stephen Orlovsky were told by their parents they must leave at once. For almost six years they hid out in basements, cellars, attics, sheds, barns, forests, wherever they could find food and meager shelter. The last bit of advice from their father was to trust no one. Isaac, the elder brother, was to be in charge. Stephen, two years younger, was never to question him.

After receiving a blessing from the elder of the synagogue

and the cantor, the boys set off along a seemingly interminable escape route which was to lead them through Eastern and Western Europe. Their youth, their innocence, their naiveté, saved them on numerous occasions. Their wit, intelligence, cunning, and courage saved them the rest of the time.

When the boys finally arrived in Chicago, the uncle they thought would receive them had either moved away or died. No one knew of his whereabouts. Hearing of the brothers' extraordinary escape, a local Jewish family took the boys into their home. From the first minute with the Rosenfelds, the Orlovsky boys felt like part of the family. Isaac Orlovsky, who had been seventeen years old when he fled from Poland, was now almost twenty-three. No one needed to tell the young men they would never see their parents again.

Exactly ten blocks from the Rosenfelds on Chicago's West Side lived Hershel and Bessy Hornstein. Rose, the middle of their five children, was several years younger than Isaac and Stephen Orlovsky. She developed a crush on both boys the moment she first laid eyes on them. She was just beginning high school and they were slowly getting adjusted to the ways of America, taking jobs and teaching in the local Hebrew school. Stephen was the better looking of the two, but Isaac was the more gentle, and surely wiser. Quite probably Rose fell in love with both boys but liked Isaac better. The story of the brothers' escape from the Nazis, the death of their parents, their charming accents, their wide-eyed approach to the mundane Chicago neighborhoods, were too much for fourteen-year-old Rose. She would marry one of them; that was for certain. The wedding would be very soon, and nobody could complain; after all, her own parents weren't much older than she was when they got married! As it turned out, however, Rose Hornstein waited longer than her parents: She was one week beyond her eighteenth birthday when she married the gentle and wise Isaac Orlovsky.

Witnesses

One morning before Harold Gruenwald left for work, a phone call came from his mother-in-law, Rose Orlovsky. Her husband Isaac, whom everyone called Zick, had been taken seriously ill. The ambulance had come in the night and he was in the hospital in critical condition. Was she at the hospital now? Harold asked, with terror in his voice. "No," Rose answered. "I couldn't bear to go in the ambulance with him and I don't have any money in the house. Can you beat it."

"Call the police," Harold ordered.

The tone of his voice caused his wife, Rachel, to ask with concern, "What happened, what happened?"

"Call the police," Harold was shouting angrily at his mother-in-law.

"I'm too ashamed," Rose wept into the telepone. "I'm too ashamed."

Harold and Rachel picked up Rose in their car and raced to the hospital where Zick Orlovsky lay on a cart in a hall ten feet inside the door to the emergency station. Harold called me and I joined the family at once. Examined immediately upon his arrival, it was diagnosed that Zick had suffered both a stroke and a heart attack. Nonetheless, for reasons that no one could explain, he lay by himself, untreated, for over an hour before receiving medical attention. At two o'clock that afternoon, Zick Orlovsky died in a room off the main hall of the emergency station. There was nothing the doctors could do, we were told. The mix-up was unforgivable, they agreed, but even the best of medical attention could not have saved Zick. Essentially he was dead when the ambulance men picked him up that morning.

"He was dead then," Rose repeated the words weakly.

"I'm afraid so," the attending doctor answered softly.

"It's like being clinically dead, is that it, Doctor?" Harold asked.

"That's exactly what we would say, Mr. Gruenwald," the

doctor replied, perhaps hoping that this term would ease the pain of Rose Orlovsky's loss. Harold did his best to comfort Rose, who was now so badly shaken she could not stand unaided.

"He was clinically dead already, Mamma," Harold said over and over agin. "They did all they could."

He appeared surprised by his own calmness, for he had loved Zick Orlovsky. Zick had wanted him to make more of himself. He had made this clear to Harold without belaboring the point. While Rose talked at the drop of a hat about the lack of ambition in the Gruenwald household, blaming both Harold and her own daughter, Zick seemed willing to live and let live. After all, who was he to talk about success? The proof of his failure to achieve, he would tell Harold, lay in the fact that neither his wife nor his two daughters knew what he did for a living.

True enough, nobody in the Orlovsky family could accurately describe Zick's work at Mening Hardware. "It was in one of the smaller warehouses," Rachel would say. "He did something with windows." Harold was equally vague about how Zick passed his working day. When the family sat shiva and several men from Mening came to pay their respects, Harold wished he could ask them what his father-in-law had done for a living.

At the moment of Zick's death, Harold revealed a sense of control he had never experienced before. He knew all about Zick Orlovsky's meager financial situation, and how his limited means might have affected the care he had received in the hospital. The poor, he would tell me later, get it in the teeth from the moment they're born to the moment they die. He remembered his father talking of death with honor. What a pitiful phrase. Death with honor was something only the rich knew. For the poor it was just a saying, an attempt to make things temporarily better. Survivors must not feel that their friends and loved ones hadn't gotten the best deals in life. What a laugh, Harold would remark. He might not have shown the highest ambitions, but people were wrong to think that he led his life ignorant of the indignities the poor were forced to endure.

"He was already clinically dead," Rose Orlovsky was muttering half to herself, half to anyone willing to listen.

"Please, Rose. They did all they could." Whatever else he might have been feeling, Harold feared a scene. Rachel was waiting outside in the lounge, unable to witness her mother's grief. "Please, Mamma Rose. Come on, we'll go home now."

"No! I want someone to explain what that means, clinically dead."

"It means," the doctor started kindly, "that while the heart is still beating, the body is not functioning. The brain isn't working, people have begun to lose or have already lost their fundamental capacities."

Harold was pleased the doctor had not patronized his mother-in-law. But he worried that perhaps Rose still would not understand, and we would have to stay in the crowded hall with the medicinal smells, listening like medical students, to the doctor's explanations. But Rose Orlovsky understood every word.

"If he was clinically dead, Doctor, then how come he spoke to me so clearly? Ask the ambulance men, they heard him."

"What did he say?" Harold seemed eager to know.

"He told me not to worry, that he wasn't going to die, that he felt weak, that was all, that I shouldn't call you and Rachel, and that I shouldn't forget to call the Budwigs to say no cards on Thursday night. My husband played cards every Thursday night, Doctor. He was so clinically dead he remembered his appointment and wanted to make certain I called Mr. Budwig. Is that what you mean by clinically dead?" Rose's voice had grown stronger.

"I'll tell you what clinically dead means, Doctor," Rose continued. "It means that when a man like Isaac is brought into this hospital from a poorer neighborhood and is taken to emergency instead of to an operating room directly, people know he's not a rich man, so he doesn't get a rich man's medical attention. That's what clinically dead means. It means you size up his pocketbook along with his medical problems when you make your decisions what to do, isn't that right, Doctor, or is my information too slanted by what they show on the television? Do you honestly believe people like us think we get the same treatment as rich people? You really think we're *that* unintelligent that we don't even *know* what we're missing out on? Don't patronize me, Doctor, with words like clinically dead. Isaac was a man, not a medical case. He wasn't dead when he left our house this morning. I heard him speaking to me, and he spoke to one of your own ambulance men, too. Isn't the man's name Jackson? Why don't you ask this Mr. Jackson if my husband was so clinically dead when they carried him out this morning? Ask him if my husband didn't say to him, 'Tell me your name. I hate to be carried out of my own house by a nice strong man who I don't even know.' The man said his name was Jackson. So tell me, Doctor, look into my eyes and tell me that my husband was clinically dead when he said that."

The doctor said nothing.

"Before you speak, I want to tell you one other little thing about being clinically dead. When your brain goes with a stroke and you begin to lose, like you said, your body functions, one of the most serious of these, isn't it, is when you can't control your bladder? So if my husband was clinically dead, wouldn't he have lost that function? So why did he say to me before they took him out of the house and again when he was lying in this hall when I stood with him for over an hour waiting for someone to do something, why did he say to me, 'You know, Rose, the worst problem is I have to urinate and there's no place to do it.' Is that what you mean, Doctor, by losing your body functions?"

"I'm sorry, Mrs. Orlovsky," the doctor said softly. "I'm truly very sorry." He made no move to leave, indicating he would stay as long as any of us wished.

"You're busy, Doctor," Rose said abruptly. "Don't stand around with us. Nothing I say will bring him back. Besides, maybe around the corner is another lady waiting for someone to come to *her* husband. Who knows, maybe the reason no one came to Isaac was because someone like me was complaining to the doctor. I don't blame you, Doctor, I just want the respect that *all* people should get, whether they come here in an ambulance or a Cadillac with a chauffeur, a mink coat or a cloth coat. Don't forget the cloth coat set, Doctor," Rose whispered as Harold helped her to her feet and turned her in the direction of the waiting room. Nurses and doctors seemed to be flying past them. Then Rose stopped and turned toward the doctor.

"You want to know, Doctor, what clinically dead means?" Leaning on Harold, Rose spoke loudly so that her words should not be lost. "It means when you've lost everything, the people you love, the little bit of hope like a fool you kept every day of your life. *That's* clinically dead, Doctor. When they take your hope away from you and rub it in the ground right before your eyes, like they were putting out a cigarette. Do I make myself clear? It's when you got nothing at all and people don't care if you live *or* die. Not even *want* you dead. If they want you dead it means in some way they care. I'm talking about people *not* caring. Isaac lay here invisible. He was invisible to you. *I'm* invisible to you. That's *your* clinically dead. You'll forget it all by tonight, but you'll excuse an old lady for rambling on. It goes with being senile, and clinically dead. We talk too much, us old ladies. I'm sorry. Maybe in all your wisdom, someone will find a drug to stop us. Then we won't bother you anymore.

128

Don't forget to ask that Mr. Jackson about talking with my husband. He'll tell you. You can believe him. He's one of yours."

Isaac Orlovsky was fifty-nine when he died.

Six

Surviving: Yankel Kanter

In psychological, or more precisely personal, terms, an examination of America's poor and elderly Jews is an examination of the way life is led. And while this phrase may be defined in numerous way, it necessarily connotes exactly what it says: leading one's life, or living life. In turn, living implies enduring, surviving, making it as far as one's biological and social psychological system allow one to go. Individual lives endure, families endure, segregated human groups and eventually integrated cultures endure. "Whatever the reason for the Jewish community's desire to persist," Marshall Sklare writes, "we should bear in mind that its dominant thrust is survivalist." Solomon Grayzel proffered much the same sentiment in his *A History of the Contemporary Jews:* "A better test of a people's vitality is its ability to stand up to historical forces and to try to be true to its values no matter how much or how suddenly conditions vary."

This last statement seems especially powerful when set in the context of elderly people living in poverty. Surely a voice like Yankel Kanter's documents and bears witness to this vitality, this survivalist posture, this capacity to endure.

Yankel Kanter and his parents and grandparents were German-born. At one time, his father was a prominent member of one of Berlin's more important synagogues. Born in 1904 in a small town near Bonn, Yankel soon moved with his family to a suburban area of Berlin, where he and his brother and sister received a fine education. Yankel Kanter was twenty-four when he married Esther Planck, whose family had moved to Berlin from Stuttgart only a few years before Esther and Yankel met. Their marriage took place in the Kanter home, where the couple then resided for several months before finding their own apartment some twenty streets away. Yankel and Esther would have three children, two girls and a boy.

It was not long after the Nazis took power that families like the Kanters were taken to death camps, although at the time no one spoke of them as such. Almost at once, Yankel was separated from Esther and the children. Surprisingly, he remained united with his brother Morris and nephew Menachem in three different camps, two in Germany, one in Poland. The two men and the boy managed to survive the camp experience. A year after peace had been established in Europe, arrangements were made for them to leave for America. Their boat docked in New York, the city in which they were to settle, in February 1947.

In seven years of continuing research on America's poor Jews, I encountered no one more delightful than Yankel Kanter. During his first three decades in America, he lived alone in apartments in older buildings, apartments that, while hardly reminiscent of his Berlin home, nonetheless made him feel safe, secure. At the time that we met, he had been obliged to leave his older apartment and move into a brand-new building several miles away which provided no space for his cherished book collection. He has never stopped resenting this move, this imposition, but he stands resigned. As he put it in one of our conversations:

"You see, when you're a Jew, Tommy, by definition you're going without. You can be the richest, most successful Jew in the world, take your choice, Mr. Kissinger even. The whole world can know you, prepare sumptuous dinners for you, treat you like you were King David himself. But inside, somewhere in you, you know that while all this is going on, you're still going without. It's your spirit that goes without, when you're a Jew, because the world doesn't accept you. The world of other people trying to keep you out is part of that reminder of what you, as a Jew, must go without. Me, I'm old, I'm at the end of my life, I don't have to worry about these things. But I have my days when I wish I were living in one of these lovely places with wood walls and hundreds of beautiful bookshelves. I remember from Germany, how I would go to people's houses and see the most beautiful libraries. No one had books in less than three or four languages. German, of course, French, English, maybe Spanish or Italian or Russian. I remember how beautifully bound they were. I remember, too, how the finest books were always kept in glass cabinets. Somebody, a maid or a butler, must have cleaned the glass once a day. There wasn't a speck of dust on them. In all the homes I visited, not a speck of dust.

"You want to know what I always planned to build if I had money. On that wall"—Yankel suddenly turned in his chair and pointed directly across from where I was sitting. A small couch covered with a silver metallic fabric stood against the wall and a narrow mahogany bric-a-brac shelf hung above it. Next to the shelf was a reproduction of a painting by Monet of the cathedral at Rouen. "On that wall, I was going to build floor-to-ceiling shelves with glass doors. No couch, no picture, nothing but shelves. Then, when all my books went in there, I was going to find one of those old wooden library ladders, you know what I mean, and put it there so people could climb up and look around for the books they wanted. I love the feeling of just imagining that bookcase. I love the idea of crawling up the ladder with the single purpose of fetching a couple books you want to read, or read again. With such bookshelves, I would never have gone out of this apartment. I wouldn't care what was changing in the neighborhood, or who lived upstairs or downstairs. I would have had my library, they wouldn't have seen me again. Not my brother, Morris, not my nephew. You, maybe, could have come in and checked out a book once in a while. Maybe I would have had some cabinets underneath for newspapers and magazines. It's funny, people come in and see you with a pile of newspapers, they ask, what do you keep all those for? That much fish you're going to wrap? But don't you read good articles in the newspapers once in a while, Tommy, that you don't want to throw away? They don't have a lot of fine people writing in the newspapers that maybe out of a little respect to them you'd like to keep a sample of their work? The same is true with magazines, no? Most of the articles I read I would like to save. But where do you save them in a tiny place like this? You can store only so many things under your bed.

"I have to smile. The man who thought up this building, *designed* it, if you can imagine someone really designing a building like this one, he knew nobody with money would live here. Now, in my old place, which once was a lovely home, there were some nice rooms. They even had real wood in there. Then I come to this place, because the good place, naturally, has to be torn down because it doesn't pay to have poor people living in a good place when you can keep them in a place like this. I'm not complaining, mind you, I'm merely pointing out that, as someone who has to *live* in this place, it doesn't make sense. But this man who built this place, he doesn't stop to think that maybe *one* person who's going to live here might just have a little interest in books.

"That's the problem with this place, with all these places. They're designed with a particular conception of the *type* of person who lives here. That is one of the most horrible things about living like a lot of us are forced to live. It's not only who

133

we are, it's what these builders and architects and politicians *believe* we are that makes me angry. What do the poor want, they ask themselves, but they never bother to ask the people who might know the answers. Well, they don't need a dining room, and they don't need much of a kitchen. What they do need is a good bed and a good toilet. You can come into these apartments, any one of them, and you hear these designers' minds working. Maybe we shouldn't give them a bathtub because we could save a little money and sleep good knowing no one's going to drown. Or maybe they'd slip getting in the bathtub or getting out of the bathtub and break a bone and we all know how old people's and poor people's bones don't heal so fast or so well as rich people's bones. But let's see, do these old poor types like to stand in the shower or would they be afraid? Maybe they wouldn't like so much water on their heads. Believe me, I'm not exaggerating. I come into this house at night I hear the ghosts of these designers. Moishe, we shouldn't have given them a bathtub. So let me ask you, with all the *thought* that must have gone into this building, like all eight minutes of it, why, if they decided on bathtubs, did they not put one thing to hold on to while you're getting into it *or* out of it? You think maybe somewhere in their minds they want us to croak in the bathtub or break our skull on the floor? And why so little cabinet space in the kitchen which means we can't do a lot of shopping because there's no way we can store food? They *want* us to go shopping every day and maybe slip on the ice in the winter? No brains. I hate to call any person stupid, but that's no brains. And you know who built this place? A man named Rosenberg. Marvin or Melvin Rosenberg. Huh? A Jew, from Germany, I'm sure. You think he lives in a place like this? You think even if he could have a penthouse on the top floor of this building he'd want to live here? Not a chance. If he lives within twenty miles of this spot I'll buy his house *and* this apartment building.

"But that's not the point. The point is that all these

builders, the Rosenbergs and the O'Briens and the Vallachis, they *make* people poor with their conceptions of poor people. They design us homes and neighborhoods which make us poor. Bathtubs or showers? You think it crosses their mind that one person in all of these apartments might one, like to read a book or newspaper once in a while, and two, might like to have a place in his home, you hear what I'm telling you, where out of the way of his normal living, he could keep a book or a newspaper? No. Give the poor a television set and a wonderful aerial so they can't complain about double and triple and quadruple vision which they already have from their bad eyesight, and you'll make them happy. I know in my heart that's what they think. You know what they think of people like us? We're cows! Give them grass to eat, they're happy. What grass is to a cow, that's television for us. So we can sit like animals watching the nonsense they put on television. So this way they keep us quiet and their own consciences quiet at the same time.

"I'm not complaining. Believe me, I'm not complaining. I'm only pointing this out. I admit, I'd love to have had money during the years when I had the strength and energy to do something with it. But I don't feel owed. On the contrary, I feel beholden. All I have this country gave me. The Rosenbergs of this country included. I got because people felt it was unfair what happened, and they wanted to give me life again, which is what they did. So I appreciate. Every bit of it. Even the small kitchen without the cabinets and the bathtub without the handles. Listen, I break my spine getting into or out of that bathtub, who'd pay for the operation if I needed one, or the hospital? The same people who gave me this. So in the end they protect me. They look out for me, and for this I am a most appreciative man. No one appreciates more than a Jew getting these things, particularly at the time we got them, and particularly now as I'm getting too old to change anything in my life. It's the conception of the *poor* family, or the poor single person. That's what bothers me. I suppose you can tell that, yes?"

As our friendship deepened, Yankel and I talked about a great many things, although never once about the fate of his family in Poland. He is in his way, although *he* would never say this, a scholarly and learned gentleman whose immediate response to almost any question of mine was: "You know, just the other night I was reading a book on that very subject." While he never could seem to remember the author, title, or publisher of the book, if one gave him several minutes to root around the stacks of books cluttering his bedroom, he would reappear with a volume in his hand and an expression of supreme satisfaction on his face. Invariably, he would say with a chuckle: "This isn't exactly the book I wanted to show you, but it's a better one even. Did you and I ever talk about Roosevelt's Cabinet? You know Harry Hopkins, of course. . . ."

Yankel could always make me laugh. Probably because he had interrogated me on my training in psychology, he constantly joked about topics like senility, forgetfulness, slips of the tongue. One day, as we talked over a cup of tea which was so weak that all I could taste was hot water and milk, Yankel said with a shamefaced smile: "You want to know something, I think I was so concerned about remembering to put milk in the tea for you but not sugar, I may have forgotten to dip the bag. You think I'm senile? I forget the tea, I can't find a single book in my bedroom and I scream when these idiots at the library have the books on the shelves misnumbered and now and again I forget where I put my socks. Between you and me, I have wash-and-wear shirts, right? So, with all the nonsense I stick in my mind, and with all the not nonsense I try to keep out of it, half the time I can't remember with those shirts is it time to wash them or wear them."

Yankel knew as well as I did that he was not senile. He knew, too, that I was waiting for our friendship to get close enough so that he might speak of the past, if only long enough to let me know the fate of his wife and children. Yankel had moments with me when his eyes showed an uncharacteristic squint, the corners of his mouth dropped, and unconsciously he would reach up to see whether his nose was running. It was as if a tracing of the past had broken through from the mysterious interior where the past is safeguarded. Then, when the moment had passed, and his face relaxed, he would glance at me, aware that I had been staring at him. I would watch him intently, letting him know that whatever he wanted to say, I was eager to hear. I never dared tell him anything as foolish as that it would be better for him to let the pain out. With a man like Yankel, one did not speak in terms of what was best for him.

Yankel knew perfectly well that he rarely did the right thing for himself. "You know," he said to me one day, "you're a very discreet person. There's a lot of things you don't ask me which you could. I'm a big boy now. I could tell you I don't want to talk about those things. I could tell you, 'Don't push so hard, psychologist, because if you push too hard you'll never hear another word from my lips.' But you don't ask. You don't ask about a lot of things. Take, for instance, when I'm sick. Like today I have a cold. You could ask me, Yankel, do you see a doctor? Do you go regularly? Do you have medical insurance? Has anyone examined you today? Has a doctor even examined you since you came to America?"

"Yankel!" I interrupted. "It can't be that in thirty years you haven't seen one doctor?"

"Why can't it be that I haven't seen a doctor? The Supreme Court just passed a law that says people have to see a doctor? It could be that I haven't seen a doctor since 1947? Since I was born for that matter? It doesn't happen to be the case, but it could be. This time, yes, I saw a doctor. A little too young for my taste, a little too much long hair, a little too much overrespect, probably more for my accent than my age, but a doctor. A genius, too. A positive genius. I didn't ask, but a genius like this has to be from Harvard. He tells me, 'You got a bad cold. What are you doing about it?' That's a genius, no? Who else but a genius could talk like that?

"Last time I got sick, I didn't go to a doctor. I stayed here. You know Fanny who doesn't come in to clean more often than she does? It must have been a full moon and Tishabov at the same time, because Fanny comes in. She takes one look at me and says, 'No, no, no. This time you have to see a doctor.' '*Nu*, Fanny, you got a great one for me?' She has to, I tell myself, she herself is either sick all the time or telling me about one of her eighty-five thousand friends who are always sick. You know what she says? 'How would I know a doctor? You got to be rich to know a good doctor.' 'But you're always sick, Fanny,' I told her, 'or you're holding the hand of a sick friend, or schlepping someone off to a hospital somewhere. How is it that you, the Queen of Medicine, doesn't know a good doctor?' I figured, what the hell, if I'm dying, I'm dying, I might just as well go out with a good laugh, although don't think I wasn't worried about who I would tell my story to if I was dead.

"So this Fanny— do you know that I can never remember her last name—she was furious with me. She's deeply insulted, like a fire gone wild. 'Mr. Kanter, Mr. Kanter,' she's huffing at me, like suddenly she's Molly Picon standing in the middle of the stage about to give the speech that made her famous the whole world around. 'Mr. Kanter, I would have a good doctor if I had money but how can I be expected to have money when people like you pay me so little to clean their apartments?'

"Fanny, Fanny, great love of my life,' I told her, 'raise your price. I can afford it. Everybody around here can afford it, then you'll have money. But if you'll accept a little piece of homey advice, you could make a little more money, a lot more money for that matter, if you'd come to work regularly. How can you collect anything when instead of working twenty even twenty-five hours a week, you don't work that much in a month? Maybe in two months for all I know!' I was just trying to help. But this woman starts shaking with rage. There she was, standing over there, right near the bed, not certain whether to come near me, hit me, walk away, jump out of the window, and the tears are starting to flow. 'Mr. Kanter, Mr. Kanter,' she's crying at me. 'I can't work every day because I'm sick. If I weren't sick I'd work, but I can't so I don't have the money and that's why I don't have a good doctor.'

"Now, *you're* a psychologist, *you* tell me what I should have said. What I *wanted* to say was, hold on a minute, I have a wonderful book right here on logic. You'll read it quickly, it's only eighty pages, you can read that in three years, then you'll come back having mastered the relationship between doctors, money, work, and cleaning apartments. That's what I *wanted* to say. Instead, I ended up telling her exactly what she wanted to hear in the first place. 'You're right, Fanny. I can't disagree with you. But you know that I *wish* you had a good doctor to recommend to me.' If you ever hear of one, let me know, okay? Maybe in one of the houses where you're working, you'll overhear someone speaking about a good doctor and you can make a mental note of his name."

"But Yankel," I said, not without some hesitation, "weren't you putting it on a bit too heavy? What's the worst it can be? She drinks maybe, doesn't work, doesn't have money, or she gets money from somewhere. I mean, she really got to you."

"That's true," he answered, sitting up straight in the brown easy chair. "I knew she had. But there were two things going on. First, you see, she had aroused this self-destructive quality I know I have, and that my brother Morris has, and my nephew Menachem has, too. Worry, worry, worry about everyone else but meanwhile let yourself go to hell. That should be a familiar story for someone in your line of work."

"All too familiar," I whispered.

Yankel sighed. "It's a funny thing. For some reason I felt in my heart that Fanny *did* know a good doctor, and for all sorts of reasons was afraid to give me that doctor's name. Maybe it was because if I met him I'd find out something strange about her, or because then I'd learn that secretly she was very rich, which of course she wasn't. Although, you never know. A great many refugees came to this country with not a small amount of money. I don't know exactly the details, but they managed to salvage a lot of what they had. But they came here and they saw how poor their fellow refugees were and they felt ashamed. So they lived like they were poor, and they took jobs, like being a cleaning lady, so others would think they were poor. You have to think, if Fanny Boehm (Boehm—that's her name) wanted money, why the hell did she clean for people like me? I had a lot of money to give her? Or a good job? Or things lying around the house she could use, like old dresses? She never once looked at one of my books. I would have been delighted if she had. She could have taken them out of here by the truckload. So you stop and think, maybe she *was* one of these rich poor ladies.

"Anyway, whatever the reason, I felt in my bones she had a doctor. And she did. The night I had that conversation with her, three hours, no more than that, after that woman with the illogical logic walked out of my house, comes a knock on the door. Who is this at five in the afternoon? And why after ten years of no visitors, which is an exaggeration since I always have several visitors a week, does someone have to come on the one day when to get out of bed to answer the door means I'm going to die from a heart attack? Suddenly the door opens, and in comes a lovely gentleman, like he should have been in England, not Manhattan. 'Excuse me,' he says, 'I'm Dr. Marlowe. I got into your house with Fanny Boehm's key which she said I should leave with you and I'm supposed to examine you.' You want the end of the story?"

"Of course."

"I'll make it short because it's not very long. Dr. Marlowe gives me a thorough examination, he prescribes medicine, returns a half hour later with the medicine, says he'll send me a bill which he never does, even after I sent him a letter requesting a bill, the medicine gives me relief in less than twenty-four hours, really, and I'm fine. Better than fine. That's the story. And that's Fanny for you. My mystery cleaning lady. But do you think the next time I saw her I asked about that Marlowe doctor? Not a half a word. Everybody has secrets, why shouldn't a cleaning lady who's supposed to clean once a week but who you're lucky to see once a month have hers? So all the story needs is a moral."

"Moral or not," I chipped in, "you don't take such great care of yourself, Mr. Kanter."

"Well, maybe I *am* self-destructive, or maybe I feel death is behind me, not ahead. All the death I want to know is back there." He waved his hands toward the window where the late afternoon light was beginning to dim. "You can worry about your own death, even be terrified of it, but in the end, if you'll excuse the expression, how can you feel your own death? You feel sad, maybe, about your own death? But do you mourn yourself? Do you go to your own funeral? Some people live as if they were going to their own funerals. But to *experience* death is to experience someone else's death, and especially someone you care about. When you lose a parent, that's bad enough, but this you expect. And you know *they* expect it for themselves as well as for you. A wife, or husband, yes, that happens, too, only it's not supposed to happen until the end of your life. But a child, a child less than a year old, no, this should never be.

"How many, Yankel?"

"Three. But the details don't matter. What's the difference, one, two, three, nobody, your whole family. You want to write about me, you should go ahead and write about me, but tell them the details don't make any difference. It's the living you're concerned about."

"It's the living you're concerned about," I offered, "but it's the dead you think about, when you let yourself."

"You're speaking now like a psychologist or a rabbi? You

want to read my mind or you want to get me to pray? Don't worry, I pray regularly, if you call ten seconds for God and twenty minutes trying to remember their faces praying. Not one photograph, not one letter. Not one piece of something that one of my children drew on or wrote on. In an old suit, down deep in one of my pockets, I discovered it two or three years after I came here, a piece of paper which obviously had come out of Germany with me. I remember my heart raced as I pulled it out and saw by the wrinkles it was old, that it came from there, from that time. I wanted it no matter what it was. It was a big piece of paper, too, not a piece of ordinary stationery. Something substantial, I thought. In this chair I sat down to read it. I unwrapped it like it was going to contain the secret of life. What did I hope for? An old letter from my wife? My daughter wrote me once, maybe this was it, this note on unfamiliar-looking paper.

"There were only two lines. The name of a woman and an address in Leipzig. The woman I never heard of, the street I knew, although it was not near where I lived. So what did I feel? I felt sad, and I felt, I think, relieved, too. I wished it had been something, a souvenir, a something that would make me know them again, but it was good it wasn't. It was best, maybe to be rid of all the material parts of the past. Bad enough you have yourself, your memory. That's enough of a souvenir. I must confess, I wrote this woman in Leipzig and asked her what her name might have been doing in my pants, but I never heard from her. Who knows, maybe I loaned my suit to a friend. Maybe it was never my suit in the first place. Who can remember what your clothes looked like? Maybe it was a mistake at a cleaning shop. Could be anything. Fanny would probably know." Yankel smiled. "Fanny, Fanny. My own little savior. Who are you, Fanny, that you decided one day to fetch a doctor for me, and how come such an elegant one? Fanny, could you by any chance, on the side, I mean, when you're not cleaning . . .? No! Unthinkable! But Fanny, you saw this Dr.

Marlowe. You must have because he got the key from you. How do you like this? I have new mysteries to deal with."

Yankel looked at me hard. "You know it's a funny thing about Jews. No matter how bad they have it, they always manage to find someone who has it worse than they do, or someone they think has it worse. Most people think all Jews do is look around to see who's doing better, who's got it better. A new car, a mink stole, a big house, being famous. But that's not all there is to it. Jews also find people who have it worse. Abe Rosen finds Sam Fishman, Sam Fishman finds me, someone else finds Abe, someone else finds the man who found Abe. We all reevaluate who we are when we look at others who are suffering more than us. But there's something more when Jews are involved, particularly the sort of Jews living around here who'll never be wealthy.

"The Jews know compassion, not because of any special intelligence or because they've read something or practiced something. They know it because they've known so much suffering. There have always been Nazis in the world. In my time they were in Germany and Poland and Austria, in another man's time they were in Spain and France. Dreyfus knew about Hitler? All the Jew has ever known is a force built with the same philosophy that National Socialism talked about in my day. The idea is to exterminate the Jews. Think about that. That you actually have grown men spending their waking hours figuring out how to kill Jews. This one's a doctor, this one's a lawyer, this one plays baseball. There are millions of grown-up, educated people putting their heads together to try to solve a problem. And what's the problem? How to exterminate the Jews. You don't believe it. It can't be, you tell yourself, but it is.

"But from that knowledge that people want you dead and want you to have no survivors comes the feeling that never once in your life should you look down your nose at a person because he's poor, or helpless, or even maybe that he's a little arrogant. You have to be compassionate when it comes to the Jews

143

because we're all just trying to survive. Not all of us had direct contact with the camps, but to be a Jew means to know about surviving. All the tradition, all the history, the children trying to learn the language of the Bible, the language of their grandparents, it all comes down to survival. All poor people, or people, let us say, with not so very much, know this feeling. But the poor Jew knows more besides. He knows he is the object of someone else's death wish. So he looks out for his family, his friends, his fellow Jews, and hopefully his fellowman. I don't worry like some people that rich Jews have lost their feelings. If they have, they could get them back. They got them back before, they could get them back again.

"Sam Fishman asks me all the time, 'So, Yankel, what's wrong with being poor? There's a crime against it?' But that's all just talk. Poor Sam. He hates being poor. One of these days, when he asks me that question, 'So, Yankel, it's so bad being poor?' I'm going to tell him, Sam, it's *horrible* to be poor. You think if God wanted us to be poor he'd let so many people get rich? Maybe if I told him I had just been reading a book on the subject, he'd believe me."

Yankel rubbed his forehead, pressing his fingers hard into his temples. "Tommy, I'll tell you something. I'm not sure it *is* all that great living what everyone calls the humble life. What makes it so wonderful?" Yankel's eyes were now tightly shut. "Sure it's important to be able to go without. No one can disagree with that. But you can learn about going without on a weekend. Why must the lesson last so long?"

Seven

A Child of the Holocaust: Menachem Kanter

A tragic historical event is central to the lives and personal development of many Jewish families presently living in poverty. All ethnic groups now residing in the United States have lived through the problems of immigration, the attempt to be included, economically and socially, into American culture. They understand the reality that a few will rise into the middle and higher reaches of the culture, while the majority will not. These are themes of introductory textbooks in sociology, books, movies. Indeed, the immigration, the battle for employment, status, social acceptance, a position of dignity in the new culture, is probably at the root of the part reality, part fantasy we continue to call the great melting pot. The Jews, too, are part of this immigration pattern and, as the data indicate, one of the more successful groups to come to America in terms of earned economic positions. But unique to the Jewish immigration is the holocaust, a horror in the evolution of the world, which, as we know by now, several decades later, continues to cause pain not only among individual survivors but in their families and descendants as well. It is not a metaphorical shadow or ineffectual remnant of the past; it is a reality with which some people have lived and will continue to live, a reality that will be passed on to the survivors of the survivors. It is part of the texture, the wholeness, real and spiritual of which the lives of the Jewish poor are composed.

One crucial point, however, should be made in introducing the words of Menachem Kanter. While the holocaust will forever be part of the history of the Jews, indeed the history of the world, the so-called Jewish image or identity must not be predicated solely on this devastating moment in history. The Jews are far more than their association with and incorporation of the holocaust. They are also three millennia of history, the Book of Exodus, the Inquisition. They are the inheritors of a history of joyous songs, rituals, literature, and a profoundly significant accumulation of human precepts, ethics, and values.

The voices in this volume bear witness to the rich variety of the Jewish experience. In Menachem Kanter's case, however, it is the holocaust that dominates the life; thus the following pages stand as testimony to that somber moment in history.

Menachem Kanter, son of Morris and nephew of Yankel, was ten years old when he arrived in the United States, with his father and uncle soon after World War II. He was enrolled in a New York public school speaking not a word of English and attended Hebrew school as well. His plans to enter college never materialized. At twenty-one, he married Linda Pescow, a close high-school friend, the only child of Sylvia and Hyman Pescow. They have one child, a son David, born in the Bronx, New York, where the family now lives.

Menachem Kanter was a man seemingly consumed by the sense of himself as a consummate failure. A spare man with a receding hairline and long thin fingers which made one believe he rarely worked with his hands, he exuded an air of sadness. In our conversations together he would jump quickly to the theme of personal failure and the sense of shame that failure brings to

Jewish people, although he would have said, to Jewish men. While maintaining a great respect for women, and a deep regard and love for his wife, he made it clear to me again and again that men can fail in ways that women cannot. When a man fails, he insisted, it destroys generations of families. It damages the expectations of parents, ruins opportunities for children, and makes life miserable for everyone. Women just don't have this burden, Menachem would say softly.

For Menachem Kanter, the strain of failure and the brooding unhappiness were exacerbated by the death of his mother in a German death camp. He barely remembered her, although her letters and photographs were brought to the United States when his father immigrated. While German was spoken in the house when he was a child, Menachem no longer could converse in the language, recalling only phrases and occasional words. When his Uncle Yankel spoke to him in German, he would nod, but he would understand very little. He remembered fragments of the trip to America, an argument at a Dutch customs' office over the authenticity of passports. But many of his recollections in fact are recollections of stories rather than remembrances of actual events. There was much uncertainty in his mind about the details of his escape from Germany when he was four, the homes in which he and his father, Morris, hid out, the people who fled with them. He remembered a woman who wore black dresses and insisted he call her "aunt." She cared for him and a number of other children in a nursery. He recalled a toy train and a stuffed giraffe that he believed were his, but when he left the nursery he was not allowed to take them. Because of this, he concluded that his caretaker had only pretended to be kind.

Morris Kanter and his brother Yankel remember the young Menachem as a lively, spirited boy who, when he first arrived in America, seemed to like Hebrew school and eating potato chips more than anything else in the world. With a package of potato chips in one hand and the haggada in the other, Yankel informed me, Menachem was utterly delighted. Menachem remembered nothing about the potato chips. He recalled Hebrew school as boring, but at least the building was warm, and the other boys were decent and hardworking. He remembered, too, asking his father whether his mother had learned Hebrew. Morris answered emphatically, yes. In the orthodox community in which she was raised, Anna Kanter did not attend Hebrew school, but her father made certain she and her two sisters learned to read and write the language. So, Menachem asked, if my mother learned it and she was killed, why should I learn it? He no longer remembered his father's reply.

Nor did he remember the nights as a small child, when he was unable to sleep, and his father and other people who lived in his house tried to comfort him. He would tell them he was having bad dreams and was afraid to sleep because he knew the dreams would return. They let him play and sleep wherever he wished, but the nightly terrors persisted. Then, suddenly, when he was seven, they stopped. When told of this time in his life, Menachem felt he was hearing about a stranger. Although not a scholar by nature, Menachem was a good student. He told himself he could become outstanding if he worked hard. Some-day, he promised himself, he would try to excel, but the someday never came. Again and again he was told that education provided the one chance for him to make something of his life; that there was no one in the world to give him anything; that whatever was to be earned would be earned by him. Love of knowledge, the fun of playing with ideas or numbers, was never discussed.

Morris Kanter ran a small stationery business. He had been fortunate to raise enough money to establish himself in downtown Boston, where the demand for his goods would be highest. One year after the store opened, two office buildings went into construction nearby and Morris rejoiced at the thought of more business. But his expectations were never met.

An increase in his volume of sales was more than neutralized by increases in taxes, rent, and the wholesale price of paper goods.

Menachem remembered his father working long, late hours, arriving home at eight o'clock, exhausted. Morris Kanter was never a well man. The doctors worried about his periodic fainting spells and his constant fatigue, but could determine no illness. Occasionally, on Sundays, Menachem would spend time with his father, but Morris usually needed that day to rest. When he found the energy, he preferred to pursue his great passion, checkers. Menachem's one clear memory of childhood was going with his father to the teahouse on Bancroft Street and watching Morris sit hunched over the board. In the first hour or so, Menachem was intrigued by the game, but after that, he became bored and irritable. He played with the children of the other men, but they never became his friends. Sunday was checkers, Friday nights, when Morris wasn't too tired, they went to *shul*. During the kaddish Morris looked weepy and Menachem fought off mingled feelings of sadness and boredom. Going to *shul* made him want to speak to his father, but he could never get clear in his own mind what he would say if they ever found the proper moment for conversation.

If one word could describe Menachem Kanter's childhood, that word would be cold. There were many nights in the small apartment when he could not get warm, even under fur blankets. His left foot was always colder than the right. His nose ran and he breathed with difficulty. This coldness was more than physical. It stemmed in part from loneliness, from hours spent alone, making model planes, listening to the radio, watching the women work in the kitchen or clean the house. He could watch people work for hours. The movements of plumbers, painters, scrubwomen, fascinated him. When noise outside announced the arrival of workmen, Menachem would dash out and stand there in the cold, shivering but enthralled. No one seemed to understand this fascination. In fact, both his father and his Uncle Yankel worried that Menachem seemed excessively interested in manual labor. Menachem remembered their concern. He wouldn't have dared admit to wanting to become a plumber or carpenter. "So what *do* you want to become?" Yankel would ask him. "I'm thinking," the boy would reply. "I'm thinking." He was saying this still at sixteen.

By the year of Menachem's bar mitzvah, Morris Kanter had become a sickly man who spent most of his time in bed. His business sold, he quickly expended his savings on medical bills, the small sum he gave regularly to Yankel, an amount no one ever spoke about, and the expenses incurred by his son and various cleaning women. Although he received support from the state, there was never enough money. By the time Menachem was sixteen, his father, now in his early fifties, was gravely ill and depressed, lacking the physical and psychic energy to seek new employment. For a while he did work in a highly successful stationery shop owned by the Hayman brothers, his former competitors. But the Haymans' success rankled in the face of Morris' own failure. Worse, he sensed that he had been hired through pity and was being exploited in the bargain.

Now at sixteen, as again and again in his life, Menachem perceived his father's message to posterity as clear: Don't end up like me. In public as well as at home, Morris proclaimed himself to be the world's number-one failure. He firmly believed that even his brother Yankel, who never worked, was the more successful of the two.

Menachem begged his father not to advertise his self-image as a failed man. It can't be good for any of us, Menachem warned him. What he wished he could say was that talk of failure scared him and made him feel he was destined to end up like his father.

Something else about his father's obsession with failure disturbed Menachem Kanter. Why was it if the job with the

Hayman brothers brought nothing but self-deprecation that Morris' health had begun to improve the instant he began working? To be sure, Morris was only a salesman, and earning less than the other salesmen at that. But his health had taken a surprising turn for the good. Even a little problem with his heart seemed to disappear.

In recalling that period, Menachem told a friend: "Failure, failure, failure. That's all I heard. Half of him got better, half of him got worse, but still it felt like he was infecting me with a strange disease. But it was a funny thing. At the same time that he complained about the low salary and how he was better than the other salesmen, none of whom knew half as much about the business as he did, he raced through breakfast just like he did when he owned his own business. I wonder whether he *was* all that depressed. Sure, owning your own business is the number-one goal, and working for someone else in a low capacity is failure. Everyone knows that. Yet he was sort of happy during that period with the Haymans. He must have questioned how he could enjoy a position he viewed as a sign of failure, but he never talked to anyone about it. Maybe he thought no one would notice. God, what a difficult and complicated man!"

While quick to complain about his troubles and emphasize his limitations, Morris Kanter told no one of the sadness in his life. Friends saw him as a hardworking, tired, burdened man who had lived through a trying history. If he didn't want to discuss his life, why should they pry? What he needed, most agreed, was a woman. She didn't have to be a wife or a mother for Menachem. But a man needs a woman to tell troubles to. Morris didn't need a replacement for his wife, he needed a friend. Yankel told him this a hundred times. "You found all this out in your books?" Morris chided his brother. "Freud, no doubt, has some theory about it?"

"You don't go back," Yankel would say, "but that doesn't mean you can't go forward. Nothing means forgetting the past, as if that were possible. Sure our lives were spoiled. But we can try to make sure the next generation suffers as little as possible. Which means Menachem." Yankel never pressed the issue. He knew that eventually Morris would drag out the old argument: "It's easy for you, Yankel, you have nobody. Maybe later when he's a man with his own family, but now he's a boy."

Yet Morris Kanter's happiness did indeed come from a woman, Fanny Boehm. When his wife died, Morris made a pledge he would never marry again. Every woman reminded him of Anna; every moment with a woman, every image he saw or imagined, brought the memories back to him. There would never again be a woman, not even for Menachem's sake, as so many people gently advised him. "Of course he needs a mother," Morris would reply bitterly. "He needs *his* mother." But Fanny Boehm became a close friend. It all started innocently enough. Morris required a woman to look after the house when he still owned the stationery business. Yankel gave him the names of several women in the neighborhood who did occasional light work. Fanny Boehm was one of them despite Yankel's warnings of her unreliability. Morris cared little about who cleaned, just as long as they didn't charge much. Fanny Boehm, as Yankel promised, was thoroughly undependable. Morris would have fired her except that she convinced him that her irresponsibility was due to her frequent illnesses.

There was a sadness and loneliness about Fanny that Menachem at once detected, but she was a kind and decent woman. She was firm with the boy, and she maintained her dignity even when undertaking the most menial job. Quiet and keenly intelligent, she could reveal an unusually witty side. She spoke German and Dutch, as her own path to survival after incarceration in death camps had taken her to Holland, where she worked as a washerwoman in the home of a doctor. The doctor not only employed her but looked after her health. A victim of medical experimentation in one of the camps, Fanny was fortunate not to have died during the war and later in Amsterdam when a hysterectomy was performed on her and a large section of bowel was removed. In her early twenties, she, too, pledged never to marry, now that she could no longer bear children. The war, moreover, had killed her ambition, as it had exterminated her family. Once a serious student of art with an eye to becoming a doctor, she gave up her plans and worked as a cleaning woman. Where she lived or what she became made little difference to her. The only thing that mattered was to serve well the people who had taken good care of her.

When, exactly, the relationship between Morris Kanter and Fanny Boehm took on a more intimate tone was a matter known only by the two of them. Menachem suspected nothing until his last years of high school. His father occasionally came home late in the evenings or disappeared from the apartment on weekends, but Menachem always assumed he was playing checkers or catching up on work. But finally Morris told his son of his secret friendship with Fanny. The boy was pleased, his father embarrassed. Menachem wondered if his father planned to be married. Morris said he would never remarry. Fanny knew this and preferred it that way. They were just friends, two people with their private reasons for not wanting to be married. Yankel, however, was not to know of the involvement. Menachem promised to tell no one.

Sadly, for Menachem, what his father called "just an important friendship" did not result in Morris and Fanny spending more time with him. She never joined them for dinner, although on the rare times that Menachem attended *shul* on Friday evenings, he occasionally spotted Fanny speaking with his father on the corner near the temple. The only noticeable change was that Fanny ceased working for the Kanters, which meant that a new cleaning woman was hired. Jennifer Riley resented her work, although in Menachem's eyes she did very little of it and complained about every speck of dust in the Kanter apartment. Menachem would let her in on Saturday mornings, but when she began washing the floors, he left and managed not to return until dinner. It had never been this way with Fanny, whom he studied with fascination.

If the revelation of Morris' special friendship with Fanny made only insignificant changes in the Kanter's public lifestyle, it aroused something very deep in Menachem. Since his childhood, he was never wholly convinced that his mother was dead. Granted, he recognized his wish to deny the fact, but he had never seen concrete evidence of her death. The Nazis had taken her prisoner, and when no one heard from her again, she was presumed dead. Thousands of families had experienced the same thing. In times of war, disappearance implied death. Still, Menachem wished he could visit her grave. They could make their own pretend grave, his father told him once, and treat it as a monument to Menachem's mother. Menachem was sickened by the idea, although his father insisted that many people did just this. Not knowing the location of a relative, they simply created a grave. It can be as holy a resting place as a real grave, he entreated his son. The rabbi would confirm his story. Menachem was unmoved. Either they found his mother, or her real grave, or they did nothing.

Without the existence of a grave, it was only natural that Menachem grew up believing in the possibility that his mother was alive. As a child, he dreamed of spending his life hunting her down, just as intelligence operators spent their lives tracking down war criminals. But there was a problem, he would think, lying in bed. What if he discovered that his mother was alive and remarried, with children? What if she had forgotten about him or decided she would rather live with her new family? What if she disappeared during the war because she never really loved her husband and son? If Anna Kanter were alive, Menachem wondered, why had she not sought him out? It would have been easy for her to learn precisely where her husband and son lived. Perhaps she had tried and was denied the information. Yankel had told such stories in Menachem's presence. Perhaps Kanter was not the true family name. Perhaps Morris and Yankel only took it to rid themselves of the war memories. If Anna were alive, she would never be able to find her husband.

Menachem's reasoning went even further. Any woman, he imagined, who befriended his father or uncle could well be his mother. Afraid to upset him by suddenly returning, she nonetheless wished to be close, if only to see how he was growing up. Yankel had many women friends. And what about Fanny Boehm? In fact, there was a resemblance between Fanny and Menachem. Morris had spoken of it, but Fanny remarked on it first. She said it was the reason she felt uneasy being around Menachem. When Menachem spoke to his father about the physical resemblance and its delicate connection to his childhood fantasies about his mother, he saw his father's eyes turn moist. "Maybe," Morris said, "that's a good reason for the three of us not living together." The words were spoken softly but firmly. Menachem could tell he must not argue the point, even though he thought his father's logic to be senseless. If three people suffered from not having a family, why not live together? What was wrong with pretending they were a family. Even real families pretended. But Morris was resolute. Fanny was to be kept separate from Menachem.

Morris Kanter's special friendship with Fanny Boehm evoked still another feeling in the young Menachem. If no one knew if his mother was alive or dead, and if he was only two when she disappeared and he was put into the care of various women, and if as a child he never spent much time with his father, then how did he know for certain that Morris Kanter was truly his father? It was an unthinkable idea at one stage in his life, but Fanny Boehm's presence turned the idea into an obsession. But to whom could he speak of this matter? Certainly not Yankel, for it would threaten his uncle just as it would his father. Far-fetched though it might be, the idea seemed just possible enough to the boy to make him cry when he thought of it too long.

Once, in school, Menachem's teacher asked the students to trace back their family history by interviewing their relatives. Students without living relatives were allowed to construct an imaginary family tree. At first, Menachem was terrified by the assignment. He told his friends the assignment was foolish, but they disagreed with him. Only the young woman, Linda Drachman, with whom Menachem had become quite friendly, listened to him sympathetically. She knew little of Menachem's background, as he, like his father, was never one to speak about it. "My father has a stationery business downtown," he told her. "My mother died in the war."

Linda Drachman could see that the family tree project had upset Menachem deeply. She urged him either to tell the teacher he couldn't do it or invent a family tree. Nervous about having to raise the subject of his background with his teacher, Menachem chose the latter solution. He listed his grandparents as born in Germany. He showed his mother dead and the existence of three brothers and three sisters living somewhere in Europe. Various uncles and aunts, whom he indicated as being enormously wealthy, were residing in Canada and South America, except for his Uncle Yankel, whom he depicted as being married with three children. The evening before the chart was due, Menachem tore it up, fell on his bed and wept.

Several years later, when Linda and Menachem had completed high school and it appeared they would one day be married, Menachem admitted to his obsession with the idea that Morris was not his real father.

"Of course he's your father," Linda blurted out. "Who else could he be?"

"He could be anybody in the world," Menachem answered flatly. "Ask your mother about it."

Linda did so that very night, for she had marriage on her

mind. While the Kanters' economic status would not be a deterrent to marriage, since her own family was hardly well off, there surely would be a problem if Menachem was mentally disturbed.

Bess Drachman's response to her daughter was forceful and direct. "Nothing can be more tragic," she told her daughter, "than for a child to be separated from his mother, especially when he is very small. But when the separation occurs because the mother is dead . . . dead? When the mother's been killed in a concentration camp, then there can be no certainty about anything in that child's mind. Why should he believe anything anybody tells him about himself, or the person he's always believed was his father? Any child who's adopted wonders who his real parents are. Take yourself, for example. If *you* want to find out, you go to City Hall and look at the birth certificate with our signatures on it. I don't know, maybe they even fingerprint babies nowadays. But even if they don't, I *saw* you being born, we both saw you all the time. There's no way in the world that you aren't our real daughter. But how can Menachem know for sure about any of this. All the records were destroyed when he came to this country. Or maybe they weren't. Maybe there are records somewhere in Germany that could prove to him that his father is really his father. Many of these people don't even want to know about these things. They all think about it, but a lot of them wouldn't dare go back. And people like us and Mr. Kanter, do we have the money lying around to take a trip to Germany to go looking for records that maybe aren't even there?

"Any one of us, no matter how we grew, wherever we came from, and thank God your father and I didn't go through that experience, any of us can look at the world and say, I doubt everything. *Prove* to me that everything I see and hear and smell and touch really exists. You could go crazy thinking like this, but you could also go through life that way. Maybe we'd say a person thinking like this is a little nuts. But in a case like

A Child of the Holocaust: Menachem Kanter

Menachem's, it's natural. We *expect* it. After all, how does he know what he knows? When the Nazis took away his mother, they took away his ability to know anything for sure, maybe for the rest of his life."

By the time he reached his thirty-fifth birthday, the year I met him, Menachem was a profoundly unhappy man. There was nothing in his life he could look at and call a success. He felt blessed to have his wife, Linda. Many men, he recognized, would have been divorced by this point. He was not a good husband; he was worse as a father to David, his son. As far as friendship was concerned, there were few people with whom he could talk. Those who took a drink with him soon found his preoccupation with personal failure tedious. Men in similar financial positions, or even worse off, hardly needed to hear laments from someone else; they could offer their own. I listened to Menachem as often as I could, and watched, as the months passed, his increasing depression. Sitting together on a park bench drinking cola one day, Menachem confronted me as follows:

"So what do I do about my life?" he questioned. "It can only go downhill, if it hasn't already reached the bottom. What can be in the future? Someone's got a bunch of surprises for me when I turn forty, or how about fifty? Now *there's* a great age to be when you've made absolutely no life for yourself. What do *you* think? Like I say, I'm willing to listen. Go on, *you* tell me what I should stay alive for. I make my wife unhappy, I make my kid angry, I got nothing to say to Bess or my father, I've lost my strength, I'm being erased. You know how kids write with chalk on the sidewalk, and how maybe if they're lucky it will stay a couple of days? Then with the rain or people walking on it, it disappears? That's me. No one's doing it; it's just being done. I'm going to be forty years old in a few years, and look at me. Look what I've built for myself. What have I done but make trouble for people, or sadness? You think my father's proud of what I am? And Bess, if I bought a house for us you think that would shut her up? The hell it would. She'd be back in a week talking better clothes, better jobs, better this. There's no end to it with her.

"So I just don't see anybody that can really give me a good lecture on why I should stay alive. Do it for your kid. That's what people always say. They said that for years about divorce, too. You know how many unhappy people stayed together for the sake of their children when they *and* their children would have been better off if the parents had gotten a divorce? The best thing I could do for both of them would be knock myself off. She'd get remarried, and David, he'd be furious and bewildered for a while, but he'd get over it. He'd wonder about it, but he wouldn't have me around bitching and moaning. Life's not easy for him. I'll tell you something: My not having a mother has its effects on him too. He knows I resent a little him having a mother when I don't. He's got damn good reason to be angry that he gets the short end of the stick because of what happened to me before he was even born.

"But it's my fault. Okay, the Nazis were bastards, the worst sons of bitches that ever walked the earth, but how long do you hold a grudge against people you've never seen? They killed my mother, we assume, so that's it. If she'd been hit by a bus, I could hold the same grudge against the bus driver. A kid has a mother, then something happens and the kid doesn't have his mother anymore. It's almost forty years ago. Four decades! How long do I suffer over it? How long does it have to be one of the things that erases me? Take it another way. Maybe it's only partly my mother dying, maybe it's the way my father raised me. Okay, he didn't do all that great, so what, we survived. I never went hungry. I got a good enough education. I always had my own room, and just about anything I wanted. It wasn't the happiest house in the United States, but it wasn't an orphanage. I had religious training which I cared about, I'm a Jew, that's all good. So where's the trouble? Why the hell do I have to be so upset about things that happened *decades* ago?

"You go up to a soldier. The guy's just sitting there on a road. He's got his pack and his gun, the whole *shmeer* on the ground next to him. He's wearing his helmet. He hasn't shaved. Maybe he's smoking a cigarette, but he's sitting there all by himself. He doesn't even speak. Okay? Now, miles away from where he's sitting is his company. Bang, bang, boom, boom, they're fighting the war miles away from the guy. He knows where he is, where they are, and where's he's *supposed* to be, but he's not there. 'Hello, Mendel, how come you're not fighting no more?' 'Don't want to.' 'What do you mean you don't *want* to? You *have* to!' 'I don't want to. I fought, tough, day and night, now I'm tired. I'm quitting.' 'But everybody else is tired, too; they've been fighting just as hard as you and they're still at it.' 'Let 'em. I'm tired.' 'But you know what will happen to you if you stay here like this?' 'The war will be won or the war will be lost.' 'And you don't care?' 'A long time ago I did, but not anymore.' 'But you can't stay here. It's against the law.' 'So they'll try me and shoot me.' 'Mendel, you're a coward.' *There's* the big punch line. You look down at this guy, and you frown, and you disapprove of him and you tell him, You're a Jewish coward bastard quitter. And that's me. So shoot me or let me smoke my cigarette in peace!

"That's the first part of the story. Of course I'm the soldier sitting there. But I'm also the other guy who asks him all these questions and tells him he's a coward. I'm that guy, too. I ask myself those questions every day. The guy questioning the soldier? That's the little bit of life I have left. But pretty soon the story's going to change. The war's still going to be on, and the soldier's still going to sit there, waiting to die, but the guy who comes up to him asking all those questions, *he's* not going to be there anymore. He's going to pass right by that soldier and he's going to tell himself, let the poor old buzzard die. If that's what he wants to do, it's nobody's business to try to change his mind. That's what it's come to. I don't want to talk any more about it. It's hard being *anything* when you're poor, but a lot of people do it. Some people are braver than me. I was brave for a while; four decades is a damn long time to put your strength behind something and come up empty-handed. My father never got out of the past. I'm out of it. I'm going to get out of the present and future, too. You just get tired.

"You know Temple Beth Shalom on Sheels Place? It used to be crowded most of the time, now you can go there and you're lucky if there's ten people for a minyan. Holidays people go, but mostly it's for old people. Last year, the old rabbi, a tremendous bore, he died. So the temple committee brought in this young guy, Marshall Weissenbrod. Brilliant. The guy's wonderful. You know he's wonderful because the old men hate him, right?

"Anyway, I listened to this Weissenbrod, and he was good. He spoke Hebrew with a rotten accent but that was all right. I even thought, what a shmuck I was not to become a rabbi, which was a lie because I never wanted to be a rabbi. You know what I used to think when I was David's age and I used to sit in temple? I used to think, poor kids grow up to become rabbis. Honest to God. Rich kids, I thought, learn Hebrew and study the Torah so they'll be well rounded when they become doctors and lawyers and businessmen.

"Anyway, Rabbi Weissenbrod and I had a talk. I went up to him one day after service and I asked him, can we talk? He said sure, why not? Not about what, just sure, why not? Two hours I sat with the man, a guy my age. Poor kid? The guy comes from tremendous wealth. Both his parents are lawyers. He went to law school *and* studied to become a rabbi. A lousy synagogue like Beth Shalom, it can't have any money in the treasury, and here's this fabulous guy who's got time to talk to me. So I thought, maybe I'm wrong, maybe religion's the answer. You want to know what he told me? If you're out of energy, you look for it wherever you can. Inside yourself, outside yourself. You look to your wife, you look to your son, you look to your relatives, your friends, memories, ideals, anything. And if you can't find the strength and you've honestly made the best effort you can, then you can't find the strength and no amount of sermonizing and praying will get it back for you. Okay? No mention of God. No mention of come to temple more often.

"I took his advice, the advice he gave by not giving any, and I started going to temple, once, twice, three times a week. I began reading again, doing a little praying. A lot of it came back from when I was a boy. I remembered my bar mitzvah, and the wedding ceremony, some of the blessings. I even celebrated with them in the temple for Simchas Torah. For six months I felt good. I talked to God, God talked to me."

"What'd he say, Manny?" I asked softly.

Menachem was grinning. "He said I complain too much. I *bourch* too much. Things like that. He told me to shape up or ship out. *My* God's a sailor, merchant marines, better." Menachem was on the verge of laughing. "Of course, no one spoke to me. I'm bad off but voices I don't hear, unless it's my mother-in-law giving lectures in the kitchen to my wife over coffee and these horrible Danish she finds from the only *treyf* bakery in the state. No, I told myself, I am what I am, I'll be what I'll be. If a man like Rabbi Weissenbrod can be so encouraging, respectful, then I don't need to look elsewhere. So I made pledges how in the New Year I'm going to be different, better. The drinker says he won't drink, the gambler says he won't gamble, the guy like me decides he'll have to live with what he has.

"So for six months it got better. Nothing changes, but maybe you feel a little bit better about yourself. You sort of stay on top of yourself. For a while it works. Then, boom, like a kid going down a slide, you go right back where you were. Down the slide, and all you think about is how poor you are, and how lousy the Jews have it, and how you hate the rich. You think about your job, and your house, and the trouble your kid's getting in to at school, and how the neighborhood's changing.

Anything can set you off. Mail comes, a bill, you get depressed. No mail, not a hello from nobody, you get depressed. And I don't think about all the dead people in my life when I'm at the bottom of the slide? I don't try to imagine my mother? It's like the slide leads you down into all the garbage of your life.

"I can be realistic about all this. I'm an unhappy man. You know that, everybody knows that. And I don't like what I am. We're poor Jewish people. We have it bad because we're Jews, and because we are not financially or politically powerful. We have no resources. Weissenbrod knows it, we all know it. When you're in this situation, which is really not that different from what the Jews face in Israel, it makes you into a child. Rabbi Weissenbrod said the same thing. We're dependent, we're dirty, we're smelly, we're like children people don't want. Not only me, every person in the temple. Go there this minute, you'll see poor children. They may be in their seventies and eighties, but they're children.

"You want to make me a man, give me a job at twenty-five thousand dollars a year, you won't hear me complain again, you won't even see me. The job and the money and I can forget the past. I'll be the kid who climbs *up* the slide. You give me the job and there's no more coming down. Rich Jews know the same feeling. Plenty rich Jews still come by Beth Shalom with their good clothes and the hundred-dollar shoes, not only during the holidays either. They remember, or they read. But *they* aren't children."

Menachem's voice had grown loud but he showed no concern that people walking in the park might have seen or heard him. He was crying, like the little boy he was trying to convince me that he was, and that he wasn't at the same time. He kept wiping his eyes and his cheeks but he never stopped talking. I said to him softly: "Come on, Manny, let's get out of here. We'll get something to eat, maybe some ice cream."

Menachem didn't budge. He sat stiffly on the bench, wiping at the tears. "You know what I feel? Like someone just told me my mother died. It's like all these years I've lived with the knowledge, but it wasn't ever a fact. Because it didn't happen in an exact minute, or an exact hour. It's like it's always been there. But right now I feel the moment of it actually came and went. Like, maybe she was alive all these years and just now I got the message."

Manny looked at me, his eyes red from crying, his hands shaking slightly, but a small smile starting to form. "This is all going to go in your book. Right? I can hear people now. What a poor slobbering fool, they'll say. So busy feeling sorry for himself, how can you have any respect for him. He's a *putz*. Climb up the slide, *putznik*, you'll see how the other half lives, how it doesn't have to be all bad. You got it bad, *putz*, but you make it bad, too. Go ahead, climb the slide. Or are you ashamed to be seen as exactly what you are. Hey, *putz*, can you look in a mirror and admit what you are? A poor Jewish *putz*. I've read enough about you to know I don't want to read any more. I'm closing the book on you, *putz*. I don't want you in my life. Go home, *putz*, cry over your mother and father, disappear, don't pester me.

"All right, story's over. We'll get ice cream. Big banana split, like a couple of kids. Come on, I'll treat *you* for a change, and for fifteen minutes we can pretend that all men are created equal."

Eight

Ambitions and Dreams: Leah Cramer

Given the commonly held impression of the Jewish community, it is difficult to believe Ann G. Wolfe was actually speaking of Jews when she wrote: "Limited education was found to be an important factor among poor Jews, half of the job seekers having less than 11 years of schooling, and one in five with less than an eighth grade education. Here, too, our blind spots operate. Because of the high proportion of young Jews in college today, and our tradition as the 'People of the Book,' we tend to overlook the earlier generation that has had a less impressive formal education."

Equally important, we tend to overlook the fact that a great many people whom we might simply dismiss today as the elderly poor once viewed their futures with the highest of hopes, confident that their ambitions would be realized. Too often we neglect to ask the elderly to share their aspirations with us, imagining, perhaps, that their ambitions, if not long since dead, linger only as the dimmest of memories.

Leah Cramer's hopes and dreams remain central to her daily experience. Hers is not a life dominated in these later years by regret, frustration over unrewarded effort, or a diminished

165

sense of self. She turns to the past not as a source of nostalgia or a basis for present dissatisfaction, but because of what it holds that is worth recounting. We know that the present makes sense only in terms of the past; like all else, to be fully understood, ambitions and dreams must be examined in temporal perspective. Who but the elderly can endow their history with this larger sense of vision?

Leah Cramer's parents were always proud to announce they were of mixed stock. Her father was part Spanish, part French, part Yugoslavian. Her mother's family was Polish and Russian. Along with several other families, the Cramers immigrated to America in the late 1880s. It is said, but not confirmed, that an entire village of Poland emigrated with them. Their boat docked in Virginia, where the families sought housing and jobs. Most of them settled there, although some went north to Maryland.

Leah herself was born in Virginia in 1896. Upon the death of her family, she moved north, taking up residence in New York, in the home of one of her mother's only relatives. She lives today in New York City, only a few blocks from the apartment once belonging to the aunt who took her in upon her mother's death, almost seventy years ago.

Leah Cramer believes that her life has been a happy and fulfilled one. Not that there haven't been sad moments; in eighty-two years there have to be. But Leah dismisses them with a smile. "Sure there were bad times, little things here and there that made me sad." But on the whole, Leah considers herself a fortunate, indeed a blessed, woman.

There were not many Jews in the little town in Virginia where Leah Cramer grew up. She recalls her father and mother occasionally going over the list of local Jewish families. This one had a baby, they would note approvingly, but that one had lost an uncle. Still it looked like there might be a few more than last year. As a child, Leah could not understand the significance of these fluctuations in population that her parents found so momentous. As long as the families of her playmates did not move away, she was perfectly content.

As for the occasional insult or barb tossed her way, these, too, seemed to matter only slightly. They came infrequently and were, in the beginning, more confusing than hurtful. One that seemed particularly peculiar was the assertion made by a girl friend that Jews don't urinate the same way as everyone else. When Leah asked her parents about it, her mother looked troubled, her father smiled. Reuben Cramer was only too aware of anti-Semitism, but when it took bizarre forms, he could only smile and shake his head. After all, what else was there to do? he would ask his anxious wife.

That Reuben Cramer was a sickly, sardonic man his daughter remembers well. He would return from his small lumber business coughing, then proceed to cough all night. In the morning he seemed better, the color in his face had returned. But with evening, the rasping cough, the ashen cheeks, a dullness in the eyes returned. Rachel Cramer said it was the combination of sawdust in the air and improper diet that was quickly killing her husband. Reuben said he could withstand the sawdust, it was the setbacks in business and continual racial slurs that were wearing him down. "They want me dead. They want me six feet under." "So we'll move, we'll start again," Rachel would tell him. To this Reuben would only nod his head. "Sure, we'll move," he'd say bitterly. "To Rome, and I'll become the Pope!"

Conversation at home was always in Yiddish, though Leah was warned never to speak that language in public. When a child came to the Cramers' small house to play, the family switched immediately to English. People claimed they loved listening to the elder Cramers speak, as their accent was charming. Leah, who spoke English like the native she was, always felt embarrassed listening to her parents. When small, she told her friends her parents were not Americans. In truth, her parents, while not American-born, had lived in the country long enough, Leah would think, that they could have learned to speak properly. She felt the embarrassment most strongly during her adolescence when she realized her parents were the butt of her friends' jokes. Youngsters would practically compete among themselves imitating the Cramers. Leah would laugh at the jokes, but inside she felt sick and angry, and her mind turned almost automatically to a long-standing wish to leave Virginia as soon as she could.

There were, of course, people in the towns in which the Cramers lived and worked who accepted them and the few other Jewish families simply as people, fellow citizens. There were also people who snubbed the Jewish families and took any opportunity to insult or openly ridicule them. These people Leah managed to tolerate. At least you knew where you stood with them. It was the group who would stare at her, their mouths literally hanging open, and then say, "You're really a Jew? We never saw one of you before. You're not that different, you know." Leah would just nod and smile, if only to help put the gawking ones at ease. When they left she might cry, or feel suddenly sick to the stomach.

Rachel Cramer was always there to help her daughter make peace with the enemy and lift Leah's mood. "You have to forget it as soon as it happens," she would counsel her only child. "You listen, you smile, you put it out of your mind. For them you're an animal in the zoo, someone they captured in the jungle and put in a cage so people can come and visit and stare at you. Maybe they expect you'll dance, and talk funny, or walk around on your knees. So they find out you're human, maybe it's an important lesson for them. Every day people have to learn a little something." Rachel's words and gentle manner soothed Leah, but the comforting always ended with the same refrain: "Every day people have to learn a little something, otherwise the day is lost. So, have you finished your lessons for tomorrow?"

It is almost seventy years since Leah heard her mother utter these words, but she has never forgotten their sound or the power behind them. Not a single school day passed without Rachel Cramer worrying about her daughter's homework. She rarely asked Leah of what the assignments consisted; her single concern was whether the girl had completed them. The child's answer was always an irritated, "Yes, Mother." No one needed to remind Leah to attend to her schoolwork. She was an outstanding student, a girl loved and admired by all her teachers. "She's always number one in everything she does," the teachers would tell her mother. "The Jewish children are just special in this way, aren't they?" "I suppose they are," Rachel would respond, glowing with pride when still another almost perfect report card was placed before her. The arithmetic could be better, she might muse, although the grade was invariably within the superior range. "Yes, it *is* something special," she would repeat, all the while thinking, is it or is it not a blessing that the child, because she's Jewish, has so few friends around here, and no brothers and sisters, she has nothing much to do with her time but study!

No matter how one explains it, Leah Cramer was a hardworking student who at an early age found the secrets to discipline and commitment. Somehow she always knew that whether or not a person was intelligent mattered far less than whether or not that person could get the utmost out of herself. Probably it was her parents' teachings that convinced her of this. How many times she had heard her parents say: "In order for us to be like all the others, we have to be better than them. If you don't understand this now, you will. You will."

None of this is meant to imply that Leah Cramer's childhood was a string of sad or bewildering experiences. Quite the contrary. She looks back on those years as a time of happiness. There were funny events, wonderful moments, mischievous and adventurous occurrences. In her words, it was a normal childhood. The danger, as she expressed it to me, "is to gaze back in time through present lenses. This is unfair. At one point in your life, you have no idea that people live differently than you. For all you know, the whole world is Jewish. And there's a point before this where being Jewish means nothing at all. Your father asks, 'Are you Jewish?' and you answer yes because he's told you to answer yes a thousand times and because he looks so proud when you do. 'Tell me, Leah, are you Jewish?' 'Yes, Dad.' It's as simple as that."

Leah recalls thinking in those early years about how certain families had more material objects than her own family. Still it didn't dawn on her that the other family might not only be richer in financial terms, but enjoying certain exclusive privileges in the community. Why should she feel deprived? There was no television; the homes on the streets adjacent to King Avenue where she lived during her early life were practically identical; her schoolmates wore clothes like hers—well, some, perhaps, were better dressed, but didn't she get the best grades?

Reuben Cramer's death when Leah was fourteen years old provided the first real test of hardship and sadness. Although she had tried to prepare herself for her husband's inevitable end, Rachel took the death very hard. He was too young, Leah remembers hearing her mother mutter over and over again, which was only too true. Reuben Cramer was forty-eight when a virulent emphysema finally overtook him. A feeling of loneliness consumed the young widow and she seemed to lose the courage and strength she had persistently demonstrated while her husband was alive. In spite of the friends who rallied around, Rachel Cramer began wasting away. She spoke a great many times of how Leah would now have to be even better at everything she did; how the family's hopes and pride now rested on the girl's shoulders. Leah could see that with all the talk and sermonizing, her mother had lost interest in living. She loved her daughter—there could be no doubt of this—and she drew strength not only from Leah's accomplishments but from her very being. Still, her life partner had died, and while she would carry on her motherly duties, her energy was low, her zest for life almost extinguished. Rachel Cramer would die seventeen months later, a week after her forty-sixth birthday.

Upon the death of her mother, Leah Cramer went to live with her mother's cousin's family in New York. Over the years, she would do some traveling, but she would never return to the state in which the first years of her life were spent. She doesn't like to talk about her brief time with the Aarons in the Bronx. While Eppie and Harry Aaron were loving people, there was no hiding the fact that they were parent substitutes. On occasion Leah would slip and call them Mother or Dad, but quickly revert back to Uncle Harry and Aunt Eppie. The Aaron children weren't much comfort. They never seemed to get used to the idea that one of the family's "orphans," as they called Leah, was a part of their household. Cousin Edith had to share her bedroom, which irritated her intensely, and while she and Leah were the same age, they managed to avoid spending much time together. The girls attended the same high school but from the first they chose different friends.

None of this, however, seemed to trouble Leah. She remained seemingly happy, did well in school, made friends easily, and handled her household tasks with efficiency. She was, everyone said, a good girl, a girl, moreover, with talent. There were many career possibilities for such a person, even though the Aarons had very little to spend on her.

Leah, too, thought of careers. Acting and music had always appealed to her, but she had another, a secret, dream. She yearned to be a business executive. She dared not mention this aspiration to anyone. Even Eppie might have scoffed at a girl from the Bronx imagining she could become a financial wizard or corporation officer.

In the various summer and after-school jobs Leah held

during her high school years, she invariably came up with new ways to improve the business. And, much to her surprise, several of her employers accepted her suggestions and put them into practice. The better her idea, the quicker the raise in her salary. More important, her employers recognized her talent and suggested she think seriously of going into some business. By the time she had completed high school, her head was filled with dreams of business triumphs, not because of the money she might earn through her contributions and initiative, but because of the challenge involved.

All of this, of course, was long ago, although when Leah recalls those days, they seem remarkably fresh and clear—not yet part of history. Sitting in her two-room apartment in the Bronx, recently painted by a high school student who has befriended her, she said:

"I have those days in my hands whenever I want them. I don't think about them as happy or sad, they were just there. I don't want anything special from them, they're not all I think about. But how can I hide the facts from myself. Sure I made a few mistakes. What should I do, lie to myself about it? What's in it for me to lie? Number one, I should have dropped everything and went to college. That's for number one, but I don't want it to sound like all I'm telling you is a package of regrets. It was a mistake. It's over, but I lived, so *something* could have been worse. Number two, I shouldn't have been such a big shot in my own head. Outside they saw me as the quiet polite girl. Inside I was already a Rockefeller. At least. I was designing businesses. Other kids were going to the movies or playing in the streets—who remembers what we did in those days? If you had a nickel, it seemed like you could go to the movies and eat and go on a streetcar somewhere. But me, I was trying to figure out how I could turn a candy store into a factory, or a linen shop into a department store.

"My first job after high school—oh, do I remember—was in the glove department of a department store that should have been torn down ten years before it was ever opened. All you had to do was go into the store to know it couldn't last. You want people to buy, you put all kinds of merchandize all over the place, pile it up high, and, this is important, let them be able to feel it, play with it in their hands. Sure they'll steal from you; they'll rob you blind, but they'll buy, too. They can't resist it once they've put it on. You know what I mean? You leave perfumes out. Customers come along and, poof, a little spritz and they'll adore themselves. They won't be able to leave it behind. Their whole personality, they'll decide, is sitting back there on that counter. If they can't steal that spritzer they'll buy it. It owns them. It's business. Everybody knows it. It's the same with shirts, blouses, gloves, shoes, all the departments I worked in one time or another. I used to tell a customer, go try it on. Once it touches their body they'll never let go of it. I have to have it. Believe me, I know the feeling. They'll save up for a million years. You put a pair of shoes in the window and a person spots them. That's all, they're hooked. They'll want those shoes and no other pair. You think we had rich people coming into that store? There wasn't a rich person within miles of the place. Poor people, working people. Money for shoes? They barely had money for food! But you put a pair of shoes in the window and you had them. They were yours, right through the glass and metal bars. It was like bait.

"So there I was, eighteen years old trying to scheme ways that would trap people into buying my goods. We had commission sales then, with a salary so low you *had* to trap those people into buying. Then we had our special customers. People like to think they have their own saleslady. 'Leah, tell me, what's come in I should see? Something different, something special.' All you had to do was look at that store and you knew nothing special or different ever came in. Half the cases were empty. Believe that? Empty! The other half had merchandise nobody would want, stuff that had been there exactly three thousand years. 'Leah, what's come in that's different, or special?' 'Ah, we just got a shipment from Paris!' What did they expect? From the store, nothing, it was all in their dreams, that's all. They dreamed *their* dreams, I dreamed mine. I was the person who connected them with their dreams, their special saleslady. 'Mrs. Pearlstein, we've just gotten in a shipment, a limited shipment of suede gloves; they're future style, if you know what I mean. They won't even be wearing these for six months, a year maybe.' Did *I* say this? To Mrs. Pearlstein? To all the Mrs. Pearlsteins of the North Bronx? To *everybody* I said it. *They* won't be wearing this style for *at least* six months! They? Who was they? Plumbers wouldn't be wearing these gloves. Surgeons wouldn't be wearing these gloves. And fashionable women, *they'd* be wearing these gloves? It was bottom of the line, imitation *shlock*, that's all, pure and simple. They knew it, I knew it, but if you don't keep the dreams alive, people themselves don't want to be alive.

"You see, in those days we didn't sit around comparing ourselves with rich people. We took what we had, knew it wasn't the best available, but lived with it. That's all there was to that. The dream of being wealthy was lived out in the buying. If you could go shopping, if you could ever tell a girl friend, come on, Sadie, let's go shopping, and she could say, good, here I'll get my wallet, which was a sign she *might* buy a little something, it meant you weren't poor; it meant you didn't have to think about what you didn't want to think about. You were going shopping and that meant you were alive, you were going to improve yourself, make yourself pretty, make yourself *better* than you were an hour ago, or yesterday. Better to yourself, better to your mother, your husband. I saw it in the way these women acted with their husbands. They didn't care if their husbands hated what they bought. And I'm not so sure their husbands cared either because hate it or love it, when they were carrying on in the store in front of a few people, what they were really saying is look at us, we're not poor, we're buying merchandise and we're arguing over whether we like it or not, we're not arguing over the price, which means we can afford it, which means we're alive; oh, we are very much alive.

"I was a business person, you see. I worked a million jobs in a million stores. One store would move me around because they knew I could sell whatever they wanted to get rid of. Then they moved me from store to store and I'd be a hit. Like a movie star. Wherever I went, I was the special saleslady. I liked it. I didn't like the standing up all day and the extra hours you worked when they managed not to give you the extra pay you were supposed to have coming to you, but it was mostly fine. I liked it because I always believed I was doing something that was substantial. I liked that word. It wasn't a big thing, and God only knows the money wasn't anything to write home about, not that I felt I had a home to write to. I wasn't that close with my cousins, although they were nice. But it was substantial. It was a living, and for a good many years I didn't give up the idea that something a touch more important might just come out of it. What it was I didn't know, but it seemed like maybe I could grow from it. I guess it never really happened. I grew a little; I sure put on the weight. I remained people's special saleslady, but I never what you could call grew. I didn't stay the same, exactly, but I didn't grow. I should have gone to college. Maybe I should have had children and grandchildren. But it didn't happen that way. There were chances, lots of chances. Gorgeous, I can tell you, I wasn't, but a disaster I also wasn't. I wasn't always fat, and I wasn't always old. I had my times.

"How close did I get to marrying Buddy Shimsky? How close? How close can you get to falling asleep without falling asleep? You can lie down, you can put your feet up, you can close your eyes, you can dream, even, and you're still not asleep. That's how close I got with Buddy Shimsky. Forty years I haven't seen him but his face is in my brain like with lights on it. Bright. He was something. Was he ever something, that nogoodnik. He and me, we'd play cards, nobody would beat us. Both of us had wonderful brains for cards. I never forgot what card was played in a game. He never forgot what card was played in every game he ever played. You can call someone like that a genius, you know. We were talents. And we danced. We danced together, alone, with music, without music. And we talked. Buddy Shimsky—his real name of course was Bernard—he could start a conversation with me—which meant, of course, him doing all the talking if I was listening or not—he could start maybe on Friday night after work 'cause we'd both work late usually on Fridays, and sometime about dinner on Sunday he'd look at his watch and say, *'Oi*, have I done all the talking? *You* talk, Leah. You talk 'cause you're a better talker.' I was, too. I *was* a better talker. I had to be. I had three hours at the most to tell him as much as I could; as much as he had told me in two and a half days. But when it was his turn to listen, he listened. The man could listen. I told myself once, Don't listen to them when they tell you how much they love you. Just ask yourself, When you talk to him, does he hear what you're telling him? If he listens, he loves, no matter what he says. Then you multiply by two: Do you listen when he talks? You do? Then you love him. I loved Buddy Shimsky. I should have gone to college: number one. Number two: I should have married Buddy Shimsky. If not, at least an affair, if I even knew what that meant in those days. Don't worry yourself, I knew. But plenty. Don't worry, too, we had plenty of affairs, Mr. Shimsky and yours truly.

"We didn't have money in those days. On Social Security now I'm almost better off than I was then, because I wanted things then and thought I deserved them. That's different from now. What do I *deserve* at eighty-two? A funeral, right, and that's as good as paid for, so I'm set. You want to know what financial security is left at my stage of life? Knowing that my death won't kill anybody else. That's it! There's a plot for me, and money the city puts aside for a funeral, so what can happen? Bergdorf Goodman won't dress the body. Who even cares then! But in those days we also didn't have money but we didn't care all that much. Sure, we talked about it. Buddy Shimsky could make lists of things he'd buy if he ever made a fortune—which wasn't going to happen so quick, I might add, selling bakery trays or whatever he did that one summer. He could make a list that would make your mouth water. Yachts, houses, cars. I could picture all of it, believe me when I tell you that. Modest I was, but tell me a little dream and I had an imagination that went to work, and I don't mind telling you worked double and triple overtime hours. But we never felt bad that we didn't have those things. I don't ever once in my life remember feeling like I could cry because I couldn't have what I wanted, a luxury item or not. But you know what did make me cry? Making a date and Shimsky didn't show. That tore your heart out, believe me. You stand and you wait and every nineteen seconds you ask somebody what the time is, and the movie's going to start and you're hungry and you're crying 'cause Buddy Shimsky with his great brain for cards, or Freddy this one or Alvin that one, could forget. Or worse than that, they could remember but good, only something better came up. *Someone* better, more likely. And you'd hear from a girl friend or one of your special customers at work Monday morning, first thing no less, how she had seen Buddy Shimsky on Friday night with Elaine Tamarack, and that hurt. Oh, you told them it didn't matter to you, there were millions of fish in the sea, but who was I kidding? Forty, fifty, *sixty* years later it still bothers me.

"Isn't that something. But that's not the point. My point is that you didn't cry over a yacht you'd never own or a gown you could sell which meant you touched it, handled it, kissed it, maybe, but you couldn't even think of buying. What made you cry until you felt your heart break was standing on the corner of Grand Concourse Boulevard there, or on Saxon Street near Van Courtlandt Park realizing the great Buddy Shimsky had stood you up and was slinking around with someone else and you were faced with the whole horrible weekend to think about and feel sorry for yourself and prepare yourself for Monday morning at nine o'clock when Mrs. Anybody comes into the store and says so matter-of-factly, 'Didn't I see you standing in front of the cinema Friday night? Did your date ever show up? What a skunk!' They were all skunks. Shimsky and all the stinkers who couldn't wait to talk to me about it at the store. And then there's this part: While I'm trying again to fight back the tears which I thought were out of me from crying over the weekend, the very same Mrs. Tattletale is leaning over the counter and telling me, 'Leah, can't you give me a little off this blouse? You get a discount, right? So tell them you're buying it for yourself and pass it on to me. They'll never notice you're buying a few sizes too small. It's a third-rate blouse to begin with, right? Like everything else they sell or can't even give away in this store.'

"I almost married Buddy Shimsky. It was close. Who knows, maybe another mistake, but it's always easy to look back, like they say. Maybe a mistake, maybe not. He told me he had some illness and I got scared. Probably it wasn't serious but I wasn't in the mood to take chances. Stand me up with other women, leave me in the rain in front of a theater miles from my house, *that* wasn't the deciding thing. He happened to mention an illness and I got scared. Having lost both my parents when they were young, maybe something in me, like a mechanism, told me to look out. How many times in a person's life, after all, does death have to make a visit? From where I stood at the time, twice was already two times too many. A psychiatrist would understand, right? So Buddy Shimsky said will you? and I said I will not. And he said how come? and I said I've got reasons. I did, too. Maybe they weren't such good reasons but they were reasons. I remember him standing in front of a cleaning shop. I think he was crying he was so upset. 'You got to have reasons,' he was yelling at me, and pleading. Believe me, he was pleading. 'I have plenty of reasons,' I told him. 'So tell me one.' And really, believe me, he was pleading. He wanted to marry me, and not just because I gave him discounts in the department stores where I worked. So now here he is pleading and crying and the tailor from the store is waving at him through the glass that he should move because we're covering up his sign. Buddy Shimsky's waving back at him like he should drop dead, so now he comes out on the street and yells at us to go fight somewhere else. Now we're laughing. Buddy's laughing with the tears and all, and in an instant I said to myself, go ahead, Leah, marry him. Forget everything, your parents, illnesses, marry him, he's a doll! Then a little voice said, you're not marrying *him*, you're marrying the scene. The tears, the laughing, and this cleaning-store man screaming at us how we're blocking his window. What did people want to look at through the window there? I wondered. To see an old man in his shirt sleeves and a vest working with an iron? That's the great sight Buddy Shimsky and I were ruining? Who knows, maybe I was ruining something far more important. But who's around to give you the answers when you need them!

"I'll tell you something, I'm not happy about what I'm talking about. I'm sounding like an old woman who does nothing in her life but look back and count the regrets. It's not true. Regrets I have, but I'm not a counter. I don't spend my days wondering how it might have been if only. I don't have enough time to waste it on that. It could have been a different life in many ways. A story that begins one way can have millions of different endings. Millions, believe me. But I've convinced myself there's a reason for life working out like it does. Someone, somewhere, there's a reason. No matter how it comes to pass, there's a reason, and people like me don't question that because it's a waste of precious time. Sure I think about all the possibilities, but I don't count regrets. I have led a very full life. I have friends, I supported myself, I never took a dime that I didn't work for. I'm a self-sufficient person. I ask nothing of nobody, although I have people who would give me. Plenty of them. I eat what I like, I have my own teeth; how many people my age can tell you that? I have my health, which, believe me, is number one. There's nothing I need I don't have. Luxury no, but everything a person needs I have. I have books, I watch my television, I have a radio, I have a man who picks up my laundry for me. I have people in this building who give me what I want. I have a birthday, I still get cards. People remember. They remember. Would you call me a *poor* woman? A poor old woman?

"People have to work at happiness, you know. They can't sit around telling anybody they meet how life played them a dirty trick. I lost my parents too early in my life, and I didn't let Buddy Shimsky and a few other nogoodniks I haven't told you about get into my life, but what am I supposed to do? Complain? Moan like an old cow? Not this kid. I figure there's a reason. God, someone has a plan, and who am I to say my piece of the plan, my role in this thing, this bigger-than-life thing, is unfair?

"Sure I get depressed once in a while, but who doesn't? Who doesn't look back at the Buddy Shimskys in their life and wonder just a little bit about them? Who doesn't wonder how else life could have gone? People in mental hospitals, maybe, don't wonder. But the rest of us do. But stay angry because you didn't have or get what others got and had, *that* I can tell you with eighty-two years of experience behind me is a waste of precious time. That *really* is standing in front of a theater waiting for someone to come when you know they're not coming. You follow my train of thought?"

Nine

Reflections and Observations

In every poor community in which I have worked, be it in Appalachia, the Midwest, the Southeast, or Northeast, I have heard the theme of genocide. In one form or another, the idea is promulgated by certain groups of people that their unlivable conditions must bespeak a desire for the collective death of the entire human group. Slavery, the death camps, and the Armenian tragedy are constantly cited as proof of the viability and utter seriousness of this ghastly concept. As Menachem Kanter once told me, "How far-fetched can it be? Look at what happened, look at what's happening. What does one need for proof!" In response to the specter of mass extermination, the young ones claim they will fight it out, or make trouble, or seek adventure, public or private, in whatever ways they can. Those in their middle years struggle on, survive, and tell me that it hasn't yet reached the breaking point; at least the government doesn't own them completely yet. With the elderly, however, the death camp sentiment, where it exists, is not so easy to extinguish. Life is reaching its final moments, and the culture seems to be doing everything in its power to hurry the passage. One cannot fight like the young ones; one does not turn so naturally to sexual powers and sexual freedom for release, as one did or might have done a few decades before. Given these conditions, what do elderly persons do or think about to maintain their equanimity and make themselves believe that, in all meanings of the phrase, they are still "holding on"?

In part the answer to these questions is found by rereading the very precious utterances of the people heard in this and all the other books where investigators have encouraged the so-called forgotten ones to be heard. It is through personal experience that people hold on and thereby remain alive. It is in their experience as well as in the need to tell their experiences that people hold on to these experiences, to the people who would listen to these experiences, and ultimately to life itself. For a story, a little vignette, "a little nothing," as Leah Cramer would forever call her lovely accounts, may very well be all that a person has, all that a person can reveal of himself or herself.

The point has a certain validity. Indeed, in the end it may be the quintessential point about the life study, especially if one considers the words of the German philosopher Wilhelm Schapp (*Philosophical Stories*, 1959): "We mean not only that we are at all times enmeshed in certain present stories, but that we are at all times enmeshed in many stories, and this being enmeshed, or perhaps having been enmeshed, constitutes our existence."

If we take seriously Schapp's rather dramatic point, then perhaps the act of collecting stories is all that the life-study researcher can do; all that anyone can do who cares to hear about another life. Surely the stories told by the elderly ones in this book represent or perhaps constitute their attachment to people and to life.

Overhearing conversations with elderly Jews reminds us of the peculiar and not wholly comprehensible status in which elderly minority people are placed in this country. It would seem in a land that consciously opened its doors to peoples of variegated origins and cultures, America has yet to resolve, in political, social, and psychological terms, its investment in the reality of immigration generally, and its immigrant cultures in particular. This is not to say, of course, that a culture predicated on homogeneous families evolving in the same land for generation after generation is by definition bland or free of profound human differences. Yet a culture like that advanced by America continues to feel the repercussions of decades of immigration. The so-called majority and nonimmigrant families feel these repercussions; so do those people who sense a peculiar closeness to their native lands, or the native lands of relatives they knew only too well. There continues to be in this culture a special status designated for individuals who are perceived as being different, and while a form of situational relevance constantly dictates the terms of how one group is different from another, we nonetheless have set for ourselves standards that all people are meant to attain if properly they may be called Americans.

Putting these various strands together, we behold the picture of poor, elderly Jews sequestered not only by their culture but in some cases by their own families. They become a subspecies, a species of humanity characterized by their differentness and their wholly unstable, even probationary status. Extending the metaphor, the poor and the elderly tend to become in our minds immigrants of a sort. Surely many readers would imagine that all the people heard in this book were born outside the United States. In fact, only a small number were. But their economic, family, religious, and, significantly, chronological status renders them different; hence we sequester them if only to build up in our attitudinal repertoire a dazzling number of misconceptions about these people. In addition, their sequestered status suggests our own complicated anxieties about aging and our most pitiable standards of relationships, often, with our ancestors. The elderly, one might suggest, do indeed live on a probationary status: Biology gives them but a limited time. But a culture remains free to choose the manner of dealing with this biological given. It may opt for one of the two antipodal extremes: namely, honor the elderly to the extent that they become almost cartoon figures, or put them away where they need never be seen or heard (of) again. Somewhere in between lies the average, expectable treatment of the elderly, which, in America, clearly needs major readjustment. As others have argued, we pay an enormous social and psychological cost by easing the elderly out of *our* normal and daily life. In social, economic, and psychological terms, divorcing ourselves first from our grandparents and then from our parents may be more destructive than the separation and eventual divorcing of marriage partners!

There is another important theme here as well: If the culture in some sense grants, though hardly in magnanimous terms, a probationary immigrant-like status to a number of its human groups, then it must have some feeling that the culture's very life has some probationary status. The culture, in other words, like its members whom it teaches, has decided that human life must be made or broken, proven or disproven, avowed or disconfirmed, within a short period of time. Like the culture, therefore, Americans may tend to see their own lifetimes as experiments, and always with time running out. Time must not be wasted, lengthy games are hazardous to our health, for time is running out; if you haven't "made it" by a young age, you'll never make it at all. Ultimately maturation comes to be defined not in terms of its etymological origins as ripening, but as aging, atrophy, and disintegration. To be mature is a deadly prescription; immaturity, while difficult to control, at least means one is still alive. To settle down and lead the so-called mature life means that one already has a foot in the grave. And if this sounds excessive, then let us suggest that even after the years of our short history, we still believe normal life cannot tolerate or accommodate the elderly. Notice we say the elderly, not the weak, the infirm, the sick, the dying. This book is not about sick and infirm, weak and dying people. Indeed, from the outset of my research, I was continually struck with the life of these people, as well as their health and vitality. As Ella Crown once remarked, "An Olympic race I'm not about to enter, but an old ladies' home where you go to die, that I'm also not about to enter!"

Several of the stories recorded in these pages are easily identified as pertaining to income, housing, employment, and other specific issues. Indeed we have underscored these themes at the onset of chapters. One theme that recurs in almost every account is that of family and kinship. Much has been said of the Jews' attachment to the concept and reality of the family. Doubtless, some have attempted to prove that the Jew is more involved with his or her family than other religious or ethnic groups are attached to theirs. I would find such attempts foolish and superfluous. The point worth noting is only that I found family attachments to be of the greatest significance to the people with whom I spoke, and hence the natural or forced detachments or uncouplings to be of the most profound significance. Clearly, many people, irrespective of age, wish to live alone. The person who chooses not to marry, not to have children, to live life in solitude, is hardly a psychopath or incipient criminal. This is not to say that many elderly people desire to live alone. Yet many, wishing not to be burdens, choose this path only to have those close to them believe this is the way they actually prefer it. If pressed to make a comparative observation on the matter—and it is really little more than an impression—I would say that of all the ethnic and religious groups living in poverty that I have studied, the elderly Jews expressed the greatest amount of criticism, not of the society that bears responsibility for their inadequate circumstances, but of their immediate and sufficiently close family members of higher social standing for simply not taking better care of them.

To make this last point rouses the very specter some of the people in this book warned me not to rouse: The Jews mustn't reveal their dirty laundry in public. Hardly liked or fully accepted by the majority of the population, the best thing Jews can do, Menachem, Ella, Willy Goldman, and Sonny Blitstein all told me in one way or another, is to keep the proverbial low profile. Lead a good life, a pure life, accomplish, make money, and stay invisible. Then *they* can say, as Sonny once told me, "Sonny Blitstein? He's Jewish? Such a handsome, nice, rich, famous guy? He's Jewish? I never knew it. Is Blitstein a common Jewish name?" Or perhaps the ideal story is that told by Johnnie Murphy, whose first and simple encounter with a Jew was touchingly memorable. Acknowledging all of these people's experiences, one can concur with their attitude and not raise the matter of those instances—and they are hardly typical—of the personal mistreatment of the elderly Jew by his or her younger and quite likely more affluent relative. Perhaps one should never publicly raise the matter of human mistreatment within groups of people still not fully accepted into the mainstream culture, as it only feeds those who would hunt for ammunition to justify their own acts of arrogance and exclusion. To pick on the Jews, moreover, is particularly precarious as in fact the Jews may have, as they say in political circles, one of the better records in the handling and care of their elderly. But there is a significant point to be made here.

The poor, elderly Jews suffer in this country precisely because they are poor, elderly, *and* Jewish. The many strange, hurtful, and utterly inaccurate slogans and assaults heard by Leah Cramer's parents in a small southern town almost a hundred years ago have not wholly vanished from the language and consciousness of America's citizens. Sadly, many people insult the Jews or perpetuate dangerous stereotypes unwittingly. I write these pages in the year 1980. Several months ago I overheard a young girl, thirteen years old, tell three friends how she had tried to "Jew" a guy down but he didn't budge. I admitted to overhearing that infamous "verb," and inquired of her whether she knew what it meant, or what its origin might be. She knew nothing of the word. Did her parents use it? I asked. No, they did not. Did her school friends use it? Sure. All the time. Did it have anything to do with the group of people known as Jews? No, there was no connection; she and her friends were quite certain of this. Finally, had she or her friends ever met a Jew? No. Well, one of them thought she might have once, but then again, she wasn't sure. The scene was a McDonald's restaurant, downtown Boston, across the street from the Boston Garden, where the Bruins and Celtics play their home games. I told this story one night to Leah Cramer. She nodded, then remarked so softly I barely heard: "You'd like to think things have changed. But no, they haven't. Still, they *must* have changed in all these years. Life can't be led without reason. All of us *have* to make a difference."

Things *have* changed; there can be little doubt of this. But within the Jewish and other ethnic communities a strain of prejudice is still felt, by all members, whether or not they choose to acknowledge it. When the Jews immigrated to America in increasingly larger waves, they received open attack. Not only varying from their European ancestors, which became still another reason to dislike or distrust them, their incorporation and presentment of so-called American values and ideals became grounds for abuse. Howard Morley Sacher writes: "They were criticized by newcomers, and some acerbic native critics, for being shallow, materialistic, secular, nonintellectual."* But notice Sacher's next point and its relationship to a point made earlier in this chapter: "This was the criticism that was leveled *at America itself* by many Europeans and some of it not without validity" (emphasis mine).† Unfortunately, if the Jews in general were made to feel only barely welcome, if they were, as we suggested, placed on a probationary status not unlike, in symbolic terms, the Ellis Island status of newcomers, then elderly poor Jews receive the abuse felt by

---

*Howard Morley Sachei *The Course of Modern Jewish History*. New York: Dell, 1977, page 540.

†*Ibid*, page 540.

other members of their own community. The family living on probationary status, the family feeling a not at all imagined sense of distrust or disapproval from the greater society, in the absence of genuine power and status offered only to those members and descendants of the main culture, will inevitably turn their reaction to this probationary immigrant-like status into self-deprecation and shame. Being the objects onto which destructive and negative attitudes are *displaced*, the minority group member is bound to displace his or her own sense of discomfort, shame, or hurt on to the next one in line. This may be another minority group person or, more likely, members of his or her own family who seemingly represent the very qualities, the main culture attributes to the Jews, or the very qualities, as Sacher observed, that Europeans attributed to America itself.

What better target of shame, self-consciousness, displeasure, embarrassment, than the elderly poor Jew who perhaps speaks only Yiddish, or English with what is still called a "broken accent," who likes the food from the *old* country (which may say something about the food in the *new* country), and who in many ways represents everything the Jew should not be if the main culture is first to accept him or her, and second, accept its own value structures and cultural ideals. Said simply, despite the existence of a widespread Jewish philanthropy, there remain the Jewish poor, some of them possibly mistreated by their own family, not primarily because of personal hostility and malfeasance, but because in a much greater historical and sociological context, the Jews have not yet been accepted in the world or in the countries they chose to adopt as their own. Thus, the weakest of their members, the most vulnerable of their group, become objects of supreme ambivalence and painful guilt to their own families. Elderly poor Jews may symbolize one's own feelings, but even more, symbolize the failing of a country to deal honorably and decently with all of its populations.

Some people, inspecting their own relatives, may just

think, if *they* ever saw my old relatives, what would they think of *me*? Will I be brought down by my old mother's or father's condition, life-style, personality, accent, breeding? Will I be punished, mistreated, or demoted by dint of the presence of these elderly people? It seems an utterly selfish and unforgivable sentiment, but if it exists, it does so because full human inclusion of the Jew has not yet been attained.

Perhaps the underlying theme of this entire study may be summarized in terms of a separation of groups of people, groups who under more noble circumstances would be living, if not together, then at least connected by a viable social tissue. Approximately 100,000 Jews entered the United States each year from 1900 to 1913. About that same number of Jews left their homelands to enter other countries during those same years. Literacy tests as forms of immigration obstacles were voted by the Congress of the United States in 1896, 1913, 1915, 1917, but presidential vetoes kept the immigration flow active. Still, in quantitative terms the numbers are small. "The numbers are always small," Menachem Kanter once advised me, "when it comes to the Jews, except when you count the suffering and the dead." In qualitative terms, the enormous separation and disconnection in social, psychological, and philosophical dynamics, which in some measure is what the diaspora is all about, is so great no single culture will ever fully comprehend it. Surely the Americans, Jews and non-Jews alike, have barely begun to articulate and integrate this continuing immigration experience, seemingly, of an entire people.

For the Jew, who feels or chooses to ignore the intellectual as well as personal ramifications of these broad and intensely complex social, historical events, something in the nature of an everyday experience must be played out. Partly this is done in reaction to the constant need to resettle oneself and one's people, partly as a way to solve the burdens, anxieties, and guilts associated with the constant reshuffling and uncoupling of people who by human right ought by now to have their homelands. The arena for this trying psychological drama, naturally, is the family, and most particularly the characters who stand for the various generations, and the experiences of these respective generations, not to mention the tensions between them. One's social class, life-style, age, or even name necessarily will carry a special added weight because of the social history of that particular human group. It goes with the territory, as the saying goes. It's an ironic expression in this one instance, since the people in question, in this country anyway, don't seem to possess much of a genuine territory. What they do possess is the territory constituted by their unique social and personal histories, a territory we have sampled in this book through a research method called the life study.

Human experience, personal as well as collective, contemporary as well as historical, comes down to the single story, the biographical or autobiographical rendering; this remains the sacred territory, no matter how profane may have been the treatment shown the teller of the story by his or her present culture or prior cultures. In the end, what makes us all great is not the particular story we might tell, but the fact that we all have a story; and the story connects us to history and to one another, even those people significantly older or younger than ourselves. The point of the story, finally, need not be that we learn about ourselves and our own particular histories when we listen to the story of another person. The point is simply that we may learn about that other person and his or her history, and that lesson may well suffice. As the Jews might say, *Dayenu:* It would be enough.